ENIGMA

How the Poles Broke
the Nazi Code

MILITARY HISTORY FROM HIPPOCRENE BOOKS

ENIGMA
How the Poles Broke
the Nazi Code

Władysław Kozaczuk & Jerzy Straszak

HIPPOCRENE BOOKS, INC.
New York

© 2004 Hippocrene Books, Inc.

ISBN 0-7818-0941-X

For information, address:
Hippocrene Books, Inc.
171 Madison Avenue
New York, NY 10016

Book design and composition by Susan A. Ahlquist, East Hampton, NY.

Cataloging-in-Publication data available from the Library of Congress.

Printed in the United States of America.

Contents

Publisher's Note

The breaking of the Enigma codes in World War II is the greatest feat of codebreaking in the history of warfare, a joint effort by the Poles, the French, and the English. While the story of British Enigma achievements (Bletchley Park and Ultra) is better known, little is known about the Polish and French contributions to the success of the enterprise. The first book to reveal that the German Enigma code was successfully broken by the Poles before the war was *Bitwa o tajemnice* (Battle for the Secrets) by Dr. Władysław Kozaczuk, published in Poland in 1967, but never published outside of Poland. Dr. Kozaczuk had the unique advantage of working with the brilliant Polish mathematician Marian Rejewski, who had made the greatest contribution to the cracking of the Enigma code.

More than half a century after the end of World War II, we still know little about the breaking of the Nazi Enigma code by Polish mathematicians even before the outbreak of the war: Few people are aware that in July 1939, just before the German invasion of Poland two months later, Polish intelligence operatives handed over to French and British representatives working models of the Enigma encoding machine and complete instructions on how to decipher the code. It was Polish mathematicians who, with help from the French, made it possible for the British to develop a singularly efficient codebreaking organization at Bletchley; it became a major weapon of the Allied defense.

Dr. Kozaczuk's account of Enigma from its creation until the fall of France in 1940 is based on his interviews with Marian Rejewski and other participants, as well as his research in Polish, German, French, and British archives and in British public records only made accessible in 1977. This particular account has never been previously published. (An earlier version, entitled *Enigma,* now out of print, had been published in America in 1984 by University Publications of America, Inc.)

Jerzy Straszak tells the story of Enigma in England, from its beginnings in 1940 until the end of the war. As a former Polish naval intelligence officer in Britain, also trained for parachute drops into occupied Poland, Mr. Straszak is very familiar with the background and literature of Ultra, which was the code name for all information gleaned from Enigma decrypts in England.

Another source of new material about Enigma, never before published in book form, is to be found in six articles drawn from the Enigma Bulletins published in Cracow by Dr. Zdzisław Jan Kapera. He has contributed a summary of international literature on the subject of Enigma, which appears as an Appendix to this book.

It is our belief that the full story of how the Allies collaborated in breaking the Enigma codes and used that knowledge to win the war will provide a true picture of the contributions made by the Poles, the French, and the British. During the Cold War, the full story of the Polish efforts could not be told; Marian Rejewski lived an anonymous life almost until his death in 1980. This book is a tribute to his memory.

We wish to express our great appreciation to Ita Straszak, the project editor, for her dedicated and sensitive guidance in seeing this collective work through to publication.

Enigma before 1940

INTRODUCTION

The breaking of Enigma was perhaps the most spectacular event, in terms of difficulty and of consequences, in the entire several-thousand-year history of cryptography (secret writing). The fact that the German Enigma machine cipher had been cracked by Polish mathematicians prior to the Second World War was first made public in Władysław Kozaczuk's book, *Bitwa o tajemnice* (Battle for the Secrets, Warsaw, Książka i Wiedza), published in 1967. Six years later, in his *Enigma, ou la plus grande énigme de la guerre 1939–1945*, France's Gen. Gustave Bertrand supplied ample corroboration for these Polish claims and highlighted the French connection with Enigma.

However, in 1974, Group Capt. F. W. Winterbotham's *The Ultra Secret*, while valuable as a source on British involvement with Enigma, made an ill-advised and since discredited claim that the British were the first to break the Enigma code. This book triggered off an avalanche of further accounts, some enlightening but many spurious.

In this manner Poland, France, and Britain documented their respective involvement with Enigma in the same order in which it had occurred historically.

1

The origins of secret writing and codebreaking reach back at least to ancient Greece and the Roman Empire. Its history is strewn with such names as Julius Caesar (inventor of "Caesar ciphers"), Gerolamo Cardano (the sixteeenth-century mathematician who first formulated certain principles of probability theory), Blaise de Vigenère (a French diplomat whose *Treatise on Ciphers* is still valued by specialists), John Wallis (the greatest British mathematician before Newton), Charles Babbage (the nineteenth-century precursor of computer theory), and August Kerckhoffs (a noted linguist who codified knowledge about ciphers up to the turn of the twentieth century).

Cryptology embraces two methods: coding, which uses short sets of figures or letters to represent whole words or phrases; and ciphering, which involves letter-by-letter substitutions. The latter system is now in general use, as it is accurate and difficult to break.

The word "cryptographer" is used to describe persons who encode and decode a message. It is also a general term for all those engaged in coding. A "cryptanalyst" or "codebreaker" is the unauthorized third person professionally engaged in researching and breaking foreign codes.

Twentieth-century cipher procedures have evolved in parallel with the general evolution of modern science, technology, and warfare. The use of telegraphy and radio in war supported and advanced the development and study of ciphers; and radio in particular was to become essential to navies and air forces that lacked other means of long-range communication.

The First World War saw important applications of cryptology for both military and political purposes. The entry of the United States into the war was hastened by Britain's decryptment of a telegram of 17 January 1917, from the German Foreign Minister Arthur Zimmermann to his ambassador in Washington. Zimmermann informed the ambassador of Germany's intention to declare unrestricted submarine warfare starting 1 February; should it prove impossible to keep the United States neutral, Germany would propose to Mexico a joint conduct of war against the U.S. A few weeks after President Wilson's publication of Zimmermann's telegram, the United States declared war on Germany.

As early as the spring of 1918, Germany's high command contemplated the use of cipher machines but, with the defeat of Wilhelm II, experiments with automatic ciphers were abandoned. The Weimar Republic was formed, and soon the notion of equipping the armed forces with cipher machines was revived and put into effect. Enigma started rather modestly as an idea for a commercial enciphering device invented by a Dutchman named Hugo Koch, who took out a patent for its design in 1919. It was a Berlin engineer, Dr. Arthur Scherbius, who in 1923 established a company to produce and market the invention that the Germans named Enigma. Scherbius's original model contained many of the basic concepts later incorporated into military versions.

The only countries that expressed interest in the machine were Germany, Poland, Japan, and the United States. Germany immediately recognized Enigma's potential for making military communications secure, introducing the latest Scherbius model into its navy in 1926, and subsequently into its ground forces. In the German army, each division had one; in the Luftwaffe, there was one in each independently operating unit; in the Navy, each ship or submarine was equipped with one. Throughout the next two decades, the machine would become increasingly complex. The number of Enigma machines that existed among the German armed forces by the end of World War II is variously estimated to have been between 50,000 to 120,000.

The first cipher machines introduced into the German forces were modified versions of the "civilian," commercial device called Enigma, which was advertised for and bought by large companies that wanted to preserve trade secrets in cipher. In 1930, a military version of the machine was constructed; the essential innovation here was a commutator, a "plugboard" with 26 connections, that—in addition to three spinning reels or rotors—vastly increased the number of possible cipher combinations. The new total was astronomical—a number that was expressed by 34 digits followed by 51 zeros. The odds of an adversary coming upon the right setting by chance were virtually nil.

The adoption of these cipher machines was part of the secret rearmament plans of the Reichswehr. The Weimar government intended to free itself of the Versailles Treaty limitations and to transform the professional one hundred thousand–man German army into a modern armed force several times that size. Even before Hitler's accession to power a decision was made to triple the number of divisions. The armored "rapid troops" and Air Force—for the time being in skeletal form—which were to become key instruments of the blitzkrieg, required efficient systems of secret radio communication by way of rapid, secure ciphers.

The German government hardly concealed its intentions to take back from Poland their "lost territories" in the east: Pomerania, the Poznań district, and Upper Silesia. The Reichswehr General Staff began drawing contingency plans for war. Meanwhile, the German covert military buildup continued and only by intelligence methods and means could it be uncovered. The Poles—rightly apprehensive over the rearming of their increasingly powerful neighbor that had been steadily increasing its military strength in violation of the Versailles Treaty (1919)—were the first to take an interest in German radio communications and ciphers. Polish cryptologists were making rapid progress between 1918 and 1928, to the point where the Polish Cipher Bureau regularly read German secret transmissions. In any case, the Poles had no choice but to keep up with the Germans who, by the mid-1920s, had broken some Polish military codes and were reading a considerable number of Polish General Staff messages.

The earliest Polish work on the intercepted Enigma signals had begun in 1928, soon after the system's introduction by the German navy and army, but practically no progress was made until 1932. At that time there were few adepts of cryptology in Poland. At the Cipher Bureau's German Branch in Warsaw, BS4, trained specialists could be counted on the fingers of one hand. The introduction by the Reichswehr of the machine cipher—which was easily recognizable by its nearly perfect dispersal of letters—was causing mounting anxiety. The unexpected appearance of a mysterious new cipher was quite a shock to the Polish cryptographers who were kept busy decoding German military messages. Suddenly new ciphers were intercepted that could not be solved by any known method, and the Poles concluded that the ciphers were machine-generated. In fact, the Enigma machine was an extremely complicated electro-mechanical system that used drums, or "rotors," for encoding. German specialists believed that nobody could read their encoded transmissions without possessing the actual machine as well as the all-important "keys" that provided the required settings. Four Polish radio monitoring stations, in Warsaw, at Starogard in the Polish "corridor," at Poznań, and at Krzesławice outside Cracow, increased their efforts to supply codebreakers with more intercepted German ciphers. But after a time there could be no more doubt: the new intricate cipher was impervious to standard codebreaking methods. Nevertheless, the Cipher Bureau, which was headed at that time by Maj. Franciszek Pokorny, did not give in.

In the meantime, the United States government became interested in Enigma and bought a commercial version of the machine in 1928. But its interest was never more than half-hearted, and shortly thereafter all official work on the machine was stopped. For as then-Secretary of State Henry Stimson, had declared elegantly, if somewhat naively, "gentlemen do not read each other's mail." Unofficially, U.S. interest in the machine continued in a tempered form.

The second foreign country to buy the machine was Japan, which used it in the Imperial Navy and the Foreign Office in a modified form—"Machine Purple," as Americans christened it. Neither Britain nor France seemed interested in acquiring the technology.

In the United Kingdom, which in the early 1930s had no success with breaking Enigma, the Government Code and Cipher School (GCCS) recruited cryptologists—ex-codebreakers who had been working in this field since World War I, and who were either retired or working in other government departments—as well as academics, mainly from Oxford and Cambridge.

Poznań

In January 1929, the director of the Poznań University Mathematics Institute, Professor Zdzisław Krygowski, had a list drawn up of those third- and fourth-year students who were fluent in German. Subsequently, selected students were asked to come to the Institute, where two officers from the Polish General Staff in Warsaw, Major Pokorny and Lt. Maksymilian Ciężki, in civilian dress, informed them that a cryptology course was being organized and invited them to participate. Twenty-odd students were pledged to secrecy concerning both the existence of the course and their own participation in it.

The choice of Poznań for the site of a course in solving German ciphers was perfectly logical. The students came predominantly from western Poland and had attended German-language schools, since the Polish language had been banned in this part of the country, which had been ruled by Prussia from the late eighteenth century until 1918.

The codebreaking course at Poznań was meant to find new cryptographic talents and to help Polish radio intelligence deal with its work against its difficult German adversary. The classes were held twice a week in the evenings, and were conducted by Cipher Bureau specialists commuting from Warsaw. Some participants who felt more at home in pure mathematics dropped out, since Professor Krygowski still required them to take their regular university examinations as scheduled. Three students, however—Marian Rejewski, Jerzy Różycki, and Henryk Zygalski, among several other young adepts of codebreaking— managed to reconcile the cipher course with their normal university work. Each of the three men contributed different talents: Rejewski, a penetrating mind and skill in advancing far-reaching hypotheses from scarce information; Różycki, elements of vivid imagination and intuition; and Zygalski, precision, energy and perseverance.

The Cipher Bureau was helped in its work on Enigma by the fact that the Polish Intelligence Service had been able to examine a commercial model of Enigma sometime in mid-1928. A box containing the machine, addressed to the German Embassy in Warsaw, had been spirited away from the Railway Customs Office one Friday afternoon, and returned before the following Monday, giving the Polish secret service the opportunity during the weekend to inspect the machine carefully. Soon afterwards the Poles legally purchased a copy of the three-rotor commercial Enigma model and set down to mastering the workings of the machine.

On 1 March 1929, Rejewski obtained his M.Phil., the degree conferred upon mathematics graduates, and received an offer to become a teaching assistant. He intended to go into actuarial mathematics, and, a few weeks later, without having completed the cryptology course, Rejewski went to Germany for a period of training in this field at Göttingen University. In the summer of 1930, having concluded the year's training at Göttingen, he returned to Poznań, ready to take up his duties as a teaching assistant.

Meanwhile, the cryptology course ended quietly. In the underground vaults of the Poznań Military Headquarters on St. Martin's Street (ul. Św. Marcina) a large room was suitably outfitted, and eight of the most promising students from the cryptology course were set to work solving German ciphers. This Poznań outpost of the Cipher Bureau, at which in the autumn of 1930 Rejewski likewise began working, afforded the young cryptologists broad opportunities for experimentation. They worked on various German codes and ciphers some twelve hours a week, selecting their own hours of the day or night. Radio intercepts were supplied by courier from Warsaw and from the nearest monitoring stations (one of which was in a Poznań suburb). The team of young codebreakers learned to exploit mistakes made by the German cipher clerks, and discovered the regular occurrence of certain code groups and letters. Indeed, by virtue of great effort and the application of such esoteric fields as permutation theory and the theory of cycles, Rejewski evolved a set of equations that resulted in a fairly rapid partial solution of Enigma codes. However, some pieces of the puzzle were still missing. Increasingly there were German military messages with which even the ablest of them were helpless.

THE ENIGMA MACHINE

In the summer of 1932, the Poznań experimental station was disbanded. Evidently the course at the Poznań Mathematics Institute, and the Cipher

Bureau outpost temporarily active there, had been set up solely in order to find talent and to train specialists to work on the Enigma.

On 1 September 1932, Marian Rejewski (who, following his return from Göttingen had for two years taught mathematics at Poznań University), Jerzy Różycki, and Henryk Zygalski (who had just graduated, being Rejewski's juniors by four and two years respectively) began work as regular employees at the Cipher Bureau in the General Staff building located at Warsaw's Saxon Square (now named Piłsudski Square).

In the latter half of 1932, Polish-German relations were particularly strained. Revanchist attacks upon Poland's western border did not cease, and in the international forum the Weimar Republic did all in its power to weaken the position of Poland, which was scornfully termed a *"Saisonstaat,"* a seasonal state. Much useful information on German diplomatic and military plans was to be gleaned from radio monitoring and codebreaking; but that was becoming harder all the time, since the Germans were increasingly using machine ciphers.

In their first weeks at the Cipher Bureau in Warsaw, however, the three mathematicians were given a new problem: a four-letter German naval code. Their work on Kriegsmarine codes was slow at first. Frequencies were drawn up for the code groups and recurring fragments were compared. But still, there was no breakthrough. A code, as opposed to a cipher, involved the substitution of symbol groups for entire words; the solution therefore rested more on linguistics and logic than on mathematics.

Finally, from a dozen short messages, one was selected for closer examination. It consisted of only six groups of four letters each. The first group, "YOPY," seemed more promising than those in the other signals. At last the reason dawned: the letter Y occurred at the beginning of a sufficiently large number of code groups to preclude chance. Were these interrogatory sentences? In German, many interrogatory expressions (*Wer? Wo? Wohin? Wann? Welcher?* etc.) begin with the same letter, and this could have been duplicated in the code.

Next, they noticed that another German station had broadcast a short signal of only four groups in response to a six-group message.

Assuming that the first message had been a question, the second might be a reply. And such a short reply, in a training message, would probably be a number.

"Four figures? Maybe it's a year? If so, then what does it refer to?"

"History? Probably, but let's not overrate the historical knowledge of our Kriegsmarine operator."

"What about, *'Wann wurde . . . geboren?'*"

"No, that's no good. It has to be six words."

"Then what about, *'Wann wurde Friedrich der Grosse geboren?'* ('When was Frederick the Great born?')"

Suddenly, everything was simple. The solution of this short signal led to the gradual reconstruction of the entire Kriegsmarine code used in the second half of 1932. For next couple of months, the Poles were able to read German naval signals. When the code was then changed, a similar effort had to be undertaken all over again. However, every week saw additions to the card files indispensable to the codebreakers. These contained such data as abbreviations of naval terms and cryptonyms for ships, their captains, ports, and naval bases on the Baltic and North Seas. The reading of a dozen or so signals pertaining to a long cruise to the Indian Ocean by a Kriegsmarine training ship augmented this information. The messages referred to equipment and places at which the ship was to call (among other places, at the Ceylonese port of Trincomalee), and so on. Even a half century later, Marian Rejewski remembered that YOPY meant "when"; YWIN, "where"; BAUG, "and"; and KEZL, "cancel the final letter."

Before work on the Kriegsmarine code was completed, the young mathematician received instructions to take up an urgent, and much more complicated problem—that of the machine cipher Enigma. "At first I worked alone in the evenings," recalls Rejewski; "I was given a separate small room in the General Staff building and instructed to renew the studies abandoned by my predecessors . . . after I had obtained the first positive results, I worked together with my colleagues, Jerzy Różycki and Henryk Zygalski."

Now, aside from approaching the code from a mathematical perspective, Rejewski had no methodological starting point. Clues had to be sought exclusively within the intercepted German ciphers, deduced from their endless, meaningless sequences of letters. The work on the enciphered texts required enormous concentration and endurance. At least eighty intercepts were collected on the same day from a monitored Enigma net, using the same setting on all its machines. At the beginning of October 1932, Rejewski was given an Enigma device of the commercial type that had been acquired in Germany. However, the Enigma, lacking the commutator with which military models of the device were equipped, solved nothing. At most, it provided a general insight into the machine's construction. It was much the same principle as the Yale lock: familiarity with one hardly enables you to open another. One still needs the key.

Externally, the machine resembled a typewriter, with an additional panel built into the lid. In the panel were twenty-six little circular glass windows bearing, like the keyboard, the letters of the alphabet; on the panel's underside were a corresponding number of glow lamps. Inside, the machine contained a set of three rotors, or rotating drums, and a reversing drum (a "reflector"), all mounted on one axle and forming part of an intricate system of wiring. The machine could be powered by a battery or by regular current passed through a small transformer.

With every stroke of a key, one or more rotors revolved. At the same time, a glow lamp beneath the panel lit up, illuminating the letter in the window above it. The machine was so designed that when one struck the keys, "typing" a plain text, the letters of the cipher lit up in the appropriate windows; and conversely, when one tapped out a cipher, the letters illuminated in turn spelled out the message in ordinary language, *"en clair."* In order to conduct a secret dialogue, both parties needed to have identical devices set to the same cipher "key" by means of various knobs and levers.

Without any knowledge of the military model of the Enigma, Rejewski had to continue studying the system on the basis of the intercepted ciphers. One of the branches of higher mathematics is group theory, concerned among other things with the properties of permutation groups; this branch of mathematics would prove especially useful in obtaining the first positive results by researching the first six letters of each message, which constituted its three-letter, doubly enciphered "key."

THE BREAK

Poland's natural allies in collecting intelligence on German armament and war plans were France and Czechoslovakia, threatened like Poland by German expansionism. Nevertheless, cooperation among the respective intelligence services depended on many factors, not least the foreign policies of the countries concerned. Notwithstanding their alliance and military treaty signed on 19 February 1921, Poland and France had frequent disagreements, therefore particularly valuable in this situation was the initiative taken in early 1931 by then-Capt. (later Gen.) Gustave Bertrand, chief of French radio intelligence. Ignoring the politicians and generals (about whom later, in the book he wrote in 1973 on the subject, he does not spare sharp criticism), Bertrand established direct cooperation with his opposite numbers in the British, Polish, and Czech General Staffs, principally on work aimed at solving Enigma. Soon he concluded that, from among the possible allies of France, the Poles had the best chance of success.

Bertrand had had good results in cracking German military ciphers during World War I, but he lacked the methods and techniques for working with rotor machines. It was his belief that the decoding of such machines could not be done by pure cryptanalysis but, rather, only with the help of the machine's plans and bought/stolen keys. His intelligence officers continued trying to develop sources for such information. The French, who never solved the Enigma machine, eventually succeeded in obtaining access to limited information about the device.

In 1932, French military intelligence could credit itself with no mean coup. It succeeded in recruiting an agent ("Asché") who worked in the Chi-Dienst, the cipher department of the German army. The intelligence supplied by Asché included some documents on machine ciphers. Unfortunately, Asché never had an opportunity to get his hands on the most important materials: the dossier on Enigma, containing the scheme of the machine's wiring, which lay in the safe of the chief of the Chi-Dienst himself.

On receipt of Asché's materials, Bertrand urgently contacted the Polish Cipher Bureau once again and arranged to visit Warsaw personally. When he arrived to sound out further possibilities of cooperation with the Poles on Enigma, he did not arrive empty-handed. But he had not expected that the materials that he brought would arouse such interest when in fact anything that extended the Poles' knowledge of the German machine cipher was welcome indeed. When Bertrand describes his meeting with the Polish General Staff officers in Warsaw, 7–11 December 1932, as "historic," it is no mere courtesy or exaggeration. Until then, the French had no direct contacts with radio intelligence chiefs and specialists from the Polish high command, except for the sporadic exchange of German radio intercepts. However, as Bertrand writes, "A reliable and durable collaboration (it was in the interest of both parties) was established, which was to be transformed into friendship and, quite unawares, entered History."

Asché's documents, while useful, were "not indispensable for the final solution of the problem, although they certainly facilitated it," according to Col. Stefan Mayer, one of the heads of the Polish Intelligence Service in the 1930s. However, the mathematician in Rejewski recognized that the intelligence contained valuable material. For though the information appeared dated—the key settings were for September and October 1932 (i.e., for two different quarters of the year)—it did provide real keys for real decoded messages sent in certain specific periods of time. When these keys were applied to old intercepted messages from Germany and combined with Rejewski's mathematical analyses, they substantially facilitated the Polish solution of the Enigma problem.

During the Warsaw meeting in December 1932, a division of tasks was established between Bertrand and his Polish opposite number, Lt. Col. Gwido Langer, the new head of the Polish Cipher Bureau, which had been thoroughly reorganized a year earlier. The French were to concentrate on furnishing intelligence from Germany that might facilitate the solving of the machine cipher, the Poles—on cryptological studies. Procedures were set up for exchange of radio intercepts, radio goniometric data (directional information relating to signals), etc. It was also decided to establish closer ties with the Czech General Staff, thereby creating a triple entente on cryptological services. This was one of the reasons why Bertrand later went to Prague. Bertrand was to use the pseudonym "Bolek" (the diminutive of the Polish Bolesław), Langer—"Luc," and the Czech officer—"Raoul." In the later 1930s, the B-L-R (Bolek-Luc-Raoul) triangle would be active in practice only on the Bolek-Luc line, owing to the unsatisfactory Polish-Czech relations obtaining at that time.

Such in barest outline was the situation toward the end of 1932 in Polish-French collaboration on German ciphers. But the actual implementers of the Enigma project, Marian Rejewski and his two colleagues, knew nothing of the Polish-French contacts at that time, or of the origin of the information supplied to them. According to Rejewski, in December 1932 he received four documents: operating instructions (*Gebrauchanweisung*) for the German cipher machine, keying instructions (*Schlüsselanleitung*), and two obsolete tables of daily keys.

The instructions brought by Bertrand gave a general idea of Enigma's structure and operating principles but said nothing about its inner wiring: about the electrical connections within the rotors, the variable contacts, or the other components. The military version of Enigma, called "E-Eins" ("Enigma I") by the Germans, as was evident from the documents signed by Lt.-Col. Erich Fellgiebel (later general and chief of Wehrmacht signals), differed fundamentally from the commercial machine. And setting E-Eins to the key, or starting position, was a complicated business. The probability of accidentally striking upon the right setting was practically nonexistent.

Characteristic of the work on Enigma was the linking by Rejewski and the two young Polish mathematicians of precise analysis with "intuitive" reconstruction. It was thanks to this that one of the important parts, the "entry ring" (*Eintrittwalze*) of the sight-unseen military Enigma, was solved. Rejewski had found that in the commercial, simpler Enigma the letters of the alphabet were represented on the entry ring in the same order in which they appeared on a German typewriter keyboard. What could be their order in the entry ring of the *military* Enigma? After many experiments that cost him much futile labor and nearly led to suspension of work on Enigma, at the end of December 1932, Rejewski took a wild guess: maybe the wiring of the ring was in alphabetical order? The hypothesis proved correct: the German fondness for *Ordnung* (order) triumphed again. Later on this important episode was aptly summed up by one of the prominent British historians in the phrase, "One lucky guess and history is changed!"

The chief breakthrough came in the first days of January 1933. The practical reading of Enigma messages began during the subsequent ten days. Success could not have been timelier. In Germany, the Nazi final campaign that on 30 January 1933 would deliver power into Hitler's hands had just begun.

An erroneous view has been reiterated in numerous publications: that the breaking of Enigma was a one-time feat, following which the cryptologists could rest on their laurels. This necessitates the following observation:

The solution of the Enigma system, which took about four months altogether, involved two distinct issues:

1. *The theoretical reconstruction of the cipher device itself.* The cryptologists first discovered the function of the reflector, or "reversing drum" *(Umkehrwalze)*, then step by step reconstructed all the connections in the machine, whose most essential components were a system of rotors (*Chiffrierwalzen*) revolving about a common axle, and the commutator (*Steckerverbindungen*) with its plug connections. This enabled the Poles to build "doubles" of Enigma that made it possible to read German ciphers, assuming that one could find the keys, i.e., the machine's initial settings prior to encipherment of a message.

2. *The reconstruction of the Enigma keys.* These cryptanalytical methods relied exclusively upon the reception and analysis of genuine, ongoing intercepts that were supplied daily by monitoring stations.

Both these problems, in all their manifold theoretical and practical aspects, were solved by the trio of mathematicians at BS4, the Cipher Bureau's German section: twenty-seven-year-old Marian Rejewski, the *spiritus movens* of the team; twenty-five-year-old Henryk Zygalski; and twenty-three-year-old Jerzy Różycki. "As for the Polish cryptologists," writes Gustave Bertrand, "to them alone belongs all the credit and all the glory for having successfully carried through this incredible technical feat, thanks to their knowledge and their perseverance, unequaled in any country in the world. They overcame difficulties that the Germans had thought to be 'insurmountable,' of which it is hard to give an idea."

ENIGMA—MADE IN POLAND

At the beginning of February 1933, the General Staff commissioned the AVA Radio Manufacturing Company at 34 Nowy Świat Street in Warsaw to build fifteen replicas of the military Enigma. The duplicates were to be made up of the same components and, by virtue of identical wiring, to work in the same way as the original military machine known to German cipher personnel as "Schlüssel-machine E-Eins."

In the feverish political period just after the Nazi takeover in Germany, the effort that had been invested in the cracking of Enigma had to be made to pay off quickly. The Polish Cipher Bureau had only one machine, and it was not the military but the commercial model, lacking a commutator. Theoretically, it was unsuitable for decrypting military signals. However, a way was found to read Enigma ciphers pending delivery by AVA of the military replicas. Caps were fitted onto the "typing" keys, and the upper part of the machine was altered, the illuminated windows being covered with cellophane on which the letters were written in an appropriate order.

AVA, headed by the brilliant engineer Antoni Palluth, was one of the first industrial plants in Poland to have its production process set up on a scientific basis. When by January 1933 the mathematicians had solved Enigma, AVA was already so far developed that, in a very short time, it was able to produce a replica of the complex German machine. By mid-1934, fifteen Polish Enigmas had been produced. A few weeks after the first Enigma duplicates had been constructed, the codebreakers received a series of German military cryptograms, which the monitoring stations noted were transmitted by districts no. 1 in Königsberg and no. 2 in Stettin. Previously effective deciphering methods proved useless in this case. Wehrmacht signals enciphered on seemingly different Enigma machines continued to come in for several weeks, then vanished as suddenly as they appeared. This was merely another in the series of Enigma mutants, which the Germans had named "E-Zwo" ("Enigma II"). Some time later, it was determined to be an Enigma equipped with eight rotors and an automatic writing device. It had been in temporary use only by highest military commands and had proved unreliable. E-Zwo's works often jammed and required complicated repairs; this was probably why it had been withdrawn from use.

In late February 1933, the world learned about the burning of the Reichstag and about the mounting terror being directed against any opponents of Hitler's new regime. In this period, the German section of the Warsaw Cipher Bureau, BS4, was augmented by a hastily trained six-person team of deciphering clerks.

During the first months after Enigma's solution, some elements of the starting positions in the various Enigma nets in Germany were obtained manually by turning the metal rotors as many as 17,576 ways, there being 263 (26 to the power of 3) possible settings. It was a tedious, time-consuming job, and on account of the work's secrecy the mathematicians could not delegate it to the technical personnel. The men's fingers, in their haste, would be scraped raw and bloody. The situation was vastly improved when Rejewski invented what he dubbed the "cyclometer." This device, based on two sets of Enigma rotors linked together electrically, served to determine the length of cycles of particular letters in German radio cryptograms. The cyclometer enabled the codebreakers to set up a catalogue of 105,456, or 6 x (26 to the power of 3), possible settings of the rotors. After that, comparison of Enigma intercepts with the catalogue gave much faster recovery of the keys. Other inventions included the "clock," devised by Jerzy Różycki, which made it possible to determine which rotor was at the far right side in a given Enigma net.

In late June 1934, the three mathematicians, although they did not ordinarily read entire signals but only broke the keys, experienced some exciting moments. As they were decrypting the beginning of a signal reading: "To all commandants of airfields throughout Germany," they surmised that this was a dramatic communication heralding important events. Further along, the message ordered the "apprehension and transportation to Berlin, alive or dead, of Oberführer Karl Ernst, adjutant to SA (Sturm Abteilung) chief of staff Ernst Röhm." Hitler, backed by Hermann Göring and the SS chief Heinrich Himmler, had just embarked on his bloody showdown with rivals within the Nazi party. On 30 June 1934, and over the next few days, the powerful Röhm, virtually all his staff, and several hundred SA functionaries died from SS and Gestapo bullets. The occasion was also taken to murder many politicians and members of opposition parties, including the former Reich Chancellor, General Kurt von Schleicher.

Thanks to the solution of Enigma, the Cipher Bureau in Warsaw could read, simultaneously with the German to whom the message was destined, many of the dispatches that were being transmitted in these tense hours and days of the German "night of the long knives." Succeeding reports spoke of further acts of terror, intensive armament, and a clandestine buildup of the army. In August 1934, with the death of President Hindenburg and the Wehrmacht's sworn loyalty to Hitler, power passed completely into the hands of the criminal dictator.

BS4 versus Chi-Dienst

In the first three years of the Nazi regime (1933–36), the strength of German armed forces increased eight-fold from about 100,000 to 800,000. After Germany's repudiation of the Versailles Treaty in March

1935, the "New Wehrmacht" was rapidly flooded with modern weapons and equipment. Numerous strong air force (Luftwaffe) and armored (Panzertruppen) units were formed. Military radio networks and signal units supplied with Enigma machines proliferated in similar fashion. At first, they comprised the two central stations of the War Ministry and a radio station at each of the seven military districts. By 1935, the number of districts had grown to twelve and subsequently increased to seventeen, while the number of divisions increased from seven to thirty-six.

The Luftwaffe Enigma network, apart from the central radio stations in Berlin, included six, later ten, air district commands (*Luftgaukommandos*) controlling numerous bomber, fighter, and reconnaissance squadrons, supply depots, and airfields.

Meanwhile, the number of intercepts was growing proportionately to the rapid pace of the Wehrmacht's expansion. A flow of reliable, up-to-date information from Germany was becoming crucial for the Polish General Staff, and radio intelligence was an essential resource. It was not enough, however, to break the Enigma system once: changes in it had to be detected and applied.

The entire prewar history of the invisible duel between Poland's BS4 decrypting center and the German Chi-Dienst, 1933–39, may roughly be divided into three periods.

In the first period, 1933–35, relatively little changed on the German side, and the methods and apparatus that had been developed by the Poles in the first few months following the Nazi seizure of power (the "grille" method, Rejewski's cyclometer, Różycki's "clock," and some others) sufficed to ensure continuous decryptment of Enigma.

In the second period, 1936 to November 1938, each change came fast upon the heels of the last one and, to keep pace with them, the Polish cryptologists had to throw their knowledge and experience into the balance, with basically the same tools at their disposal.

Finally, in the third period, from late 1938 to September 1939, there was a tense confrontation with a new generation of Enigmas, following the introduction by the Nazis of new components and further complications in encoding procedures that had been planned for total mobilization and war.

In the business of cipher- and codebreaking, as in other fields that join theory with practice, it is concrete achievements that count. And these are not ensured by even the greatest erudition and industry: imagination is also required, plus a certain amount of luck. Whatever one may call it now, fate itself seemed to smile upon the Polish enterprise and to conspire against the Nazis.

When in 1933 the most intensive work on Enigma was in progress in Poland, German cipher clerks were committing outrageous blunders. They often selected message keys (the first six letters at the beginnings of messages) in a predictable manner. For example, they would strike the same letter three times (AAA) or they would strike letters in alphabetical order (ABC). Or else, they would use letters that were adjacent to each other down or diagonally across the keyboard—which was also against regulations. The cipher personnel were probably still poorly trained and their supervision by their bosses less than perfect. But after Enigma had been broken, these German shortcomings disappeared. "So if we had set to work just a couple of months later," said Marian Rejewski, "we would have had a lot more trouble. In fact we had the impression that the Germans had got jittery, as if they sensed intuitively that something had happened."

Later, in November 1937, when the Nazis exchanged the reflector wheel in their Enigmas, they made the mistake of not changing the wiring in the three enciphering rotors at that same time. The Poles' work was also facilitated by the Nazi Sicherheit Dienst's (SD) delay in switching to new procedures of enciphering message keys that had been adopted by the Wehrmacht on 15 September 1938 (which they finally did on 1 July 1939). But the crux of the matter seems to have been the Germans' blind faith in Enigma, a belief that it could transform *anything* into an absolutely unbreakable cipher. Nonetheless, the Polish mathematicians at BS4—thanks to the cycle principle discovered by Marian Rejewski (which a German researcher has recently called a stroke of genius)—were able to react quickly and to exploit any blunder or error on the part of their adversaries.

ON THE BRINK OF WAR

With the arrival of the year 1938, international relations took a sharp turn for the worse. In February, Hitler eliminated the rather weak attempts at opposition among his generals, removing Field Marshal Werner von Blomberg and Gen. Werner von Fritsch from their high posts. The Third Reich commenced its first territorial annexations in Austria and Czechoslovakia through intimidation.

Meanwhile, in January 1938, the Polish General Staff ordered the carrying out of an experiment designed to demonstrate BS4's efficiency in reading intercepted Wehrmacht ciphers. The test, conducted over a two-week period, showed that the ten-man team of cryptologists and operators was able to solve and read about 75 percent of all intercepted Enigma messages. This was a remarkable result, considering that part of the intercepts were garbled or incomplete owing to interference.

On 10 March 1938, Hitler took the final step in carrying out Germany's *Anschluss* (annexation) with Austria, assembling along her borders an army of 105,000 men comprised of Wehrmacht troops, and newly formed SS regiments (Standarten): the Germania, the Deutschland, the Adolf Hitler guard regiment, and a Totenkopfstandarte (Death's Head regiment) come from Dachau in Bavaria. "Any resistance," proclaimed the order issued on the eve of the march on Vienna, "is to be broken mercilessly with the force of arms." The German troops were to act ruthlessly in applying military law; and the same went for any form of passive resistance. Germany's neighbors wondered: if such methods were ordered for an operation billed as a "reunion" (*Wiedervereinigung*) of sister nations, how would "unfriendly" countries be treated?

On 12 March 1938, German troops crossed into Austria along her entire border from Schärding to Bregenz, and Luftwaffe squadrons landed in Vienna. On the fourteenth, Austria ceased to exist as an independent state, and her army (Bundesheer) was incorporated into the Greater German Wehrmacht.

What were Polish-French relations like during the tense period following the Nazi occupation of Austria? They were considerably closer in radio intelligence than they were in the political sphere. Bertrand recalls

20

that, on one of his trips to Warsaw, his train stopped en route in Vienna just as German troops were entering that city. When he telephoned his superiors, proposing to stay in order to observe the *Anschluss* and collect information, he was ordered to return home at once. The French politicians had written off Austria. Eventually, the governments of France and Britain lodged a "protest" with Hitler.

It was only in May 1938 that Bertrand could once again set out for Poland. On the twenty-seventh, after several days of consultations, the Poles invited him to see the new BS4 center code-named "Wicher" ("Gale") in the Kabackie Woods near Warsaw. There, the French officer later recalled, "everything was in concrete bunkers, from the radio station to the cryptologists' offices: this was the brain-center of the organization, where work went on day and night in silence." That was Bertrand's penultimate visit to Poland. On his way home he stopped in Prague, where he spoke with representatives of the Czech General Staff, which at that time was still contemplating the future with hope.

Following Germany's annexation of Austria, the British began to show more interest in intelligence contacts with their future allies. Shortly after the *Anschluss* in March 1938, Bertrand was invited to London, where he was able to meet the British signal intelligence and cipher experts. The British cryptological service was part of the Foreign Office, although it contained some military sections. Officially known as the Government Code and Cipher School, or GCCS for short, later it was also referred to as Station X or Bletchley.

The longtime chief of the GCCS, Cmdr. Alastair Denniston, was a professional naval officer who, during the First World War, had worked at breaking German ciphers in the famous Room 40 at the Admiralty. The chief cryptologist at GCCS, Alfred Dillwyn Knox, had also worked at Room 40. It is now known that, beginning in the mid-1930s, GCCS had worked hard at breaking the Enigma machine cipher but had failed to make headway. The reason the British were stymied, aside from the methods used (about which little is known), appears to have been that they lost the race against time. The Poles, in addition to using the precise tools of mathematical analysis, had begun their research several years ahead of the British. In mid-1938 and the next tension-filled months, decrypting Enigma became of mounting concern to Britain's radio intelligence and codebreaking services, as nothing indicated that, in the event of a new war against Germany, they would be able to repeat the First World War successes of Room 40.

Meanwhile, following the destruction of Austria's sovereignty, the full fury of Nazi propaganda and subversion was directed against Czechoslovakia. A secret order from Berlin caused the Sudeten Deutsch Party (S.D.P.) to present Prague with demands for "broad autonomy" for the region. And as had been the case in Austria, a Nazi fifth column began stirring up trouble. Multiplying acts of sabotage, which the Czech authorities sought to counter, deepened the tensions and chaos in the country that had been singled out by Hitler to be the next object of aggression. On 23 September, Czechoslovakia declared a general mobilization, raising the strength of that country's armed forces to a million and a half men. France carried out a partial mobilization, while Great Britain ordered a naval alert. Underway in London were British-French talks that revealed a lack of readiness and will to resist potential German aggression firmly. On the thirtieth of that month, the Munich conference, attended by Hitler, Mussolini, Chamberlain, and French Premier Daladier, ended with the capitulation by the Western powers to the Nazi demands and the surrendering to the Reich—without any consultation of the Czech government—of the Sudeten region, complete with its vital zone of border fortifications.

From late October 1938 onward, there were clear signs that the next object of German attempts at intimidation, possibly of open aggression, would be Poland.

THE BOMBE

A peculiar, invisible game was being played out on the European chessboard. The German Chi-Dienst certainly knew that their adversary to the east existed and acted (for example, they knew the locations of the three Polish radio-monitoring stations at Starogard, Poznań, and

Krzesławice, in addition to the locations of the main French and British stations). It probably never occurred to them that, insofar as Enigma was concerned, this was strictly a Polish-German duel and that they had been losing it for several years running. In any case, so as to ensure foolproof security and deny their adversaries any insight into the Wehrmacht's war preparations, they decided on a grand castling operation.

On 15 September 1938, two weeks before the Munich conference, the Germans radically altered the rules for enciphering message keys on the more than twenty thousand Enigmas then in use by Hitler's army, air force, navy, and key civil agencies of the Reich. The stream of information that had ceaselessly flowed from Enigma to BS4 in Warsaw suddenly dried up. However, the Polish cryptologists found, to their amazement, that a readable trickle continued to flow. These interpretable signals originated from an SD (Sicherheits Dienst) radio net that continued to use the old keying procedure. But while the SD signals gave much valuable data about internal German relations, it was now essential that the Poles obtain up-to-date military information. An attempt had to be made to reestablish as quickly as possible the decryptment of Wehrmacht radio correspondence.

The changes being introduced by the Nazis created a need for further automation of decryptment. The Polish mathematicians at BS4 had long been thinking of constructing a device superior to the cyclometer to take over laborious calculations. In mid-October 1938, Marian Rejewski worked out the mathematical model of an apparatus that, after thorough checking, was turned over to designers at the AVA factory in Warsaw.

This device was christened the *"bomba"* in Polish, the colloquial meaning of the word being "splendid" or "sensational." *Bomba* ("bombe") was also the name of a popular ice-cream dessert in Warsaw, a scoop of vanilla ice cream covered in chocolate. It is said that the idea for the name came to Różycki while he was enjoying this confection. The path from the bombe plan to the finished apparatus was a short one. The components, which had been produced at the AVA plant, were brought to the German section of the Cipher Bureau, BS4, in the first ten days of November 1938 and assembled by technicians sworn to secrecy.

23

The bombe was an electro-mechanical machine based on six Polish Enigmas, combined with additional devices and transmissions. An electrically driven system of rotors revolved automatically within the bombe, successively generating, over a period of about two hours (100–120 minutes), 17,576 different combinations. When the rotors aligned in the sought-for position, a light went on, the motor stopped automatically, and the cryptologist read the indications. Thus by setting in motion multiple bombes (six were built at once in November 1938), the daily keys in different German Enigma networks that had been monitored and intercepted on a given day could be recovered within about two hours. A number of ideas that constituted the acme of existing technology were used in the bombes, such as semi-elastic axle shafts and transmission wheels, and special instantaneous glow lamps.

Almost simultaneously with the creation of the bombe, a new method was worked out for breaking the doubly enciphered Enigma keys, based on using a special series of perforated paper sheets with a capacity of 51 x 51 holes, and on manipulating the sheets so as to match the coincident places in this pre-programmed system. Designed by Polish mathematician Henryk Zygalski, the system was effective regardless of the number of plug connections in the German Enigma's commutator.

Using these new devices—the bombes and the perforated sheets—the Poles were once again able to find the keys to Wehrmacht signals. During the several months after the Munich conference, BS4 not only continued reading the SD machine ciphers but also was again solving the German Enigma-encrypted military messages. In December 1938, the Germans once again revamped their Enigma ciphers by introducing two additional rotors per device, thereby raising the number of rotors from three to five (Only three rotors operated in the machine at any one time). The SD cipher bureau received the additional rotors, the fourth and fifth, for their Enigmas at the same time as the Wehrmacht, but until 1 July 1939, they continued to use old keying methods. This lack of coordination was immediately exploited by the Polish codebreakers. They were able to research and to reconstruct the internal connections in rotors IV and V. This had opened up possibilities of again reading the secret radio correspondence of the Wehrmacht's ground and air forces, though with a much greater effort. And on New Year's Day, 1 January 1939, the Enigma picture became still murkier: as though uncertain of the efficacy of all previous measures, the Nazis now increased the number of plug connections in the Enigma commutator.

A sharp escalation had taken place in the struggle for mastery of the already war-oriented Enigma cipher system. While the system, with all its new complications, was again mastered theoretically, continuous decryptment would have required immediate possession not of six, as previously, but of at least sixty cryptological bombes and as many series of perforated "Zygalski sheets." To be sure, the sheets were inexpensive, but their programming and manual production would have required the training of many new operators, all sworn to secrecy. Concurrently with the expanding number of Wehrmacht radio nets, there was a growth in the needs of the monitoring stations, which were to be supplied with modern equipment. Also necessary was the stepped-up production of Polish-made Enigmas: to read the intercepted cryptograms, and to stockpile the devices for their anticipated use in wartime. The struggle for secrets of the Third Reich was becoming ever more expensive.

The Polish General Staff decided to broaden its exchange of information on Enigma with potential allies. Constant liaison had been maintained with the French, but the latter still did not know that Enigma had been solved back in 1933. The first meeting to be attended also by British representatives took place on 9–10 January 1939, in Paris. However, no significant decisions were then made.

The second tripartite meeting of the Allied cryptological services took place in Warsaw on 25–26 July 1939, at the initiative of the Polish government. The delegations present were composed as follows: British—Alastair Denniston, Alfred Dillwyn Knox, and "Comdr. Humphrey Sandwith" (under which pseudonym Col. Stewart Menzies, future head of Britain's secret intelligence service, may have been hiding); French—Major Bertrand and Captain Braquenié; and Polish— Lieutenant Colonel Langer, with Major Ciężki at his side, and the three young cryptanalysts, Rejewski, Zygalski, and Różycki, who were unknown to any of the guests.

The purpose of the meeting was of historic importance to all concerned. With war so imminent and in light of the facts that the British had offered immediate assistance were Polish independence threatened (March 1939), and that France and Poland had signed a mutual assistance treaty, the Chief of the Polish General Staff, Gen. Wacław Stachiewicz, authorized the Cipher Bureau to make available all its know-how and technical aids for solving Enigma to Poland's future war allies. This was to be the Polish contribution to the common cause of defense. As the Poles did not have sufficient technical resources to further their development of the bombe, they would share Enigma's secrets with their allies, Britain and France, in the interest of pooling their resources.

The moment of truth had arrived. On 25 July, the assembled men were taken to a secret forest location at Pyry near Warsaw, where the Polish cryptology center was located. Ironically, the only common language among them was German, although Rejewski spoke some French, and Zygalski and Różycki tried to make themselves understood in English. Once there, Langer revealed what he knew. He showed the guests the Polish-made Enigma and the six bombes which, when run simultaneously, provided the required answer, one which could be worked out within two hours.

Both the British and the French participants at the meeting were astounded by these disclosures. They must have thought that Christmas had come early, such was the magnificence of this gift. Each team was given a Polish-made military model of the Enigma machine, including the wiring for five rotors, as well as technical drawings of the bombe and the other cryptanalytical devices invented by the Poles. It was immediately evident that the British understanding of the Enigma was far poorer than that of the Poles, although Knox had a fairly firm grasp of the machine's mechanics. In fact, he had worked on the mathematical procedure for the daily settings of the keys but thought that solving the wiring of the rotors was not possible. He was peeved to learn that Rejewski had done it purely with mathematical calculations and rare insight. Bertrand says, "It was now, perhaps for the first time, that the pride of the British technicians was lowered by the achievement of the Poles."

Later, Knox admitted that he was mistaken in his belief that the Enigma codes could not be broken and graciously thanked the three Polish cryptographers. Enclosed in his note to each of the Poles was a beautiful scarf with a view of a Derby horse race. David Kahn, the American author of *Seizing the Enigma,* wrote that the British and the French had received that day from their loyal ally a method of solving the most guarded secret enemy information, and that the Poles had demonstrated a will and a vision that both the British and the French had lacked at the time.

Bertrand subsequently undertook the transport of the two Enigma machines given to the two Allied teams, which he carried from Warsaw to Paris in French diplomatic baggage. From the British Embassy in Paris, Bertrand took one of the Enigma machines to London, accompanied by a courier and a Secret Service man. He was welcomed by a grateful Menzies. The date was 16 August 1939—in the nick of time, as several days later German tanks crossed the Polish frontier and the Second World War began.

The Warsaw tripartite conference in July 1939 had far-reaching effects. Now the Allied high commands could also set up teams for deciphering the most secret Nazi radio correspondence. And if this had been important before September 1939, because it enabled observation of German armament and preparations for aggression, it was quite invaluable in the war years 1939–45.

WAR BEGINS

The final days of August 1939 were marked by feverish work in the German section of the Polish Cipher Bureau. In the Kabackie Woods near Warsaw, the BS4 radio intelligence center was working around the clock; the codebreakers and operators had been on three shifts since the spring of 1939. In the secluded building perfectly camouflaged in thick foliage, the bombes and Polish Enigmas clattered without pause, transforming most enemy ciphers into plain language. The fact that, in

August 1939, the Polish General Staff identified 80 to 90 percent of all the Wehrmacht units assembled at Poland's borders was due in no small measure to this decryptment center.

The day before the attack on Poland, on 31 August, SS Sturmbann-führer Naujocks, a confidant of Heinrich Himmler, carried out an operation that was supposed to furnish a *casus belli*. Hitler did not much care whether the pretext was plausible: no one would judge the victor anyway. That evening, Radio Gleiwitz suddenly interrupted its scheduled programs. A manifesto by "insurgents," calling on Silesians to "take up arms," was read in broken Polish. Shots rang out and faked sounds of battle were transmitted. About 11 P.M., the radio station resumed its regular programming. The announcer informed his audience that Poles had attempted to take over the station but the authorities had restored order and foiled the "perfidious plot." Meanwhile, along Germany's eastern border, the Wehrmacht's motorized and armored divisions were already taking up their starting positions for the onslaught.

On 1 September, at 4:45 A.M., the firing of the heavy 280-mm guns of the German battleship *Schleswig-Holstein* on the Polish military outpost, Westerplatte, in Gdańsk, announced the beginning of the Second World War. German armored divisions crossed the Polish frontier.

In addition to the well-known incident at Gleiwitz, which had been staged for political ends, the Germans employed several lesser-known stratagems meant to disorganize Polish defenses. On the second day of the war, the German naval intelligence post B-Dienst (Beobachtungs Dienst) at Swinemünde broadcast a bogus order, ostensibly from the Polish Supreme Command, for Westerplatte to discontinue resistance and surrender. The attempt failed (*"der gewünschte Erfolg blieb aus,"* notes the former head of German naval radio intelligence, Commander Heinz Bonatz, in his memoirs).

An air defense bulletin on casualties and damage in Warsaw reported that German bombs had hit the new AVA production facilities on Szczęśliwicka Street. These had been built and fitted out with modern equipment shortly before the war. Whether this was simple chance, or whether Nazi agents had picked the target in advance, was never learned. BS4 in the Kabackie Woods near Warsaw worked normally only in the first days of September. The situation at the front was getting worse daily. The thin zone of defensive positions was cracking under the massed blows of Nazi armor, and thousands of airplanes emblazoned with black crosses hung in the skies from dawn to dusk, attacking not only military units but also open cities and civilian refugees on the roads.

On 3 September, Britain and France declared war on Germany, but this did nothing to relieve the pressure on Poland. The French armed forces did not move, while Britain's Royal Air Force dropped propaganda leaflets on Germany instead of bombing troop transports and airfields.

In view of the deteriorating situation at the front, the Cipher Bureau and its German section, BS4, received an order to destroy part of their files and equipment and prepare to evacuate. All Bureau personnel were henceforth at the disposal of the Supreme Command, which had been transferred to Brześć (Brest Litovsk) on the Bug River in eastern Poland. A special evacuation train, the "Echelon F," moving slowly due to track damage, reached Brześć on 10 September. Meanwhile, German Panzer spearheads, bypassing strongly defended Warsaw, pushed on eastward, and the Polish Supreme Command soon abandoned Brześć. The Cipher Bureau's personnel and secret equipment—Polish-made Enigmas and Polish "Lacida" cipher machines—had to be kept from falling into enemy hands. The subsequent evacuation route led south-southeast through Kowel, Łuck, and Husiatyn. The news at the successive stages was increasingly alarming. Because of lack of fuel, some of the trucks had to be abandoned; equipment and documents were gradually destroyed.

The Cipher Bureau, along with other units of the General Staff, received orders to evacuate to Rumania. On the seventeenth, half a mile southeast of the town of Kuty, the BS4 cryptologists, together with other military and civilian General Staff personnel, crossed a bridge over the Czeremosz River into Rumania. At the border, a Rumanian officer separated the military from civilians and indicated a different direction of march to each group. Taking advantage of the confusion caused by the arrival of the next wave of refugees, Rejewski, Zygalski, and Różycki, who kept together, proceeded to the nearest railway station. By then, the three had lost contact with their superiors Langer and Ciężki. Avoiding an order to proceed to a refugee camp, they boarded a train that brought them directly southward to Bucharest at the other end of Rumania. There, anticipating that they might easily be identified by the Rumanian security police, which was then infiltrated by German informers, they tried, with the help of the Polish military attaché, to get in touch with the British authorities who, they remembered, had shown particular interest in working with the Poles at the final memorable meeting at Pyry. But there were delays and confusion at the British Embassy, which was busy trying to accommodate its own Warsaw Embassy staff that had been evacuated to Bucharest. The harried British officials told them to return in a few days' time. As the Poles could not wait, they sought help from the French Embassy, using the name of Maj. Gustave Bertrand as a reference. Bertrand's name acted like magic. Their case was dealt with immediately. The French intelligence service looked after them very well. In short order they gave them all the necessary documents, money, railway tickets and transit visas.

After a train's ride via Belgrade, Zagreb, and Trieste, the mathematicians reached Turin, Italy, where the Italian fascist security police, suspicious of three young men in civilian clothes, closely questioned the Paris-bound Poles. But luck was with them; their papers were found to be in order and they were allowed to proceed to France. By 25 September they found themselves in Paris. Somewhat belatedly, the British intervened and proposed that the cryptanalysts come to London, but the French refused to give them up. After all, it was they, not the British, who had been instrumental in getting the Poles out of Rumania.

Meanwhile, the majority of the BS4 personnel, including Lieutenant Colonel Langer and Major Ciężki, were taken to internment camps from which they succeeded in fleeing only a few weeks later with the help of Bertrand who had gone to Rumania to secure the release from internment camps of officers and civilian workers of the former Polish Cipher Bureau. On 1 October 1939, Langer arrived in

Paris, together with his group of fifteen cryptologists. Other specialists followed later and, in but three weeks' time, officers and specialists of the Polish Cipher Bureau had regrouped in the radio intelligence and deciphering center code-named "Bruno," located at the Château de Vignolles in Gretz-Armainvillers, about forty kilometers from Paris. The château had been transformed into a bustling, efficient radio intelligence center. Bertrand was appointed head of Bruno, responsible to the Fifth Bureau of the French General Staff; Langer headed the Polish team. Bruno and Bletchley were linked together by a teletype line across the Channel. A joint French-British radio monitoring station for intercepting German Enigma signals was created on a small island, Sainte Marguerite, near Cannes.

However, the hierarchy among the cryptologists had altered. Gen. Władysław Sikorski was forming, with numerous difficulties, a new Polish government-in-exile in France, and new regular armed forces. Arms, equipment, and barracks were scarce. A Polish Radio Intelligence Unit was organized but, for security reasons, the cryptologists were not officially enlisted. Langer's group was in exile from a defeated country and the French, as yet unscathed and on their own territory, could call the tune. The Poles, although they formed the backbone of the operation and were the most experienced in that group, became subordinate to the French, who at the time were still confident and full of optimism.

BRUNO OUTSIDE PARIS

By the end of October 1939, the Bruno Radio Intelligence Center had become operational. The center was home to about seventy cryptological and technical staff: forty-eight Frenchmen, fifteen Poles, and seven émigré Republican Spaniards working with Italian ciphers whom Bertrand had enrolled in the Foreign Legion. The Polish team took on the code name "Ekipa Z." Two French radio monitoring systems worked for its service: the Network for Monitoring and Radio Goniometry of

Foreign Radio Transmissions (Réseau d'Écoute et de Radiogoniométrie des Emissions Radio-électriques Etrangères, or REG), and the Network for Supervision of Domestic Radio Broadcasting and Investigation of Clandestine Stations (Réseau de Contrôle des Emissions Radio-électriques de I'Intérieur et de la Recherche des Postes Clandestins, or RCR). Thus, Bruno was supplied with voluminous signals traffic both from the Reich and from Nazi agents operating on French territory.

Bruno was, of course, a top-secret establishment where everyone wore a uniform and strict security measures were maintained at all times. Beginning in November 1939, the Franco-Polish Bruno center became the chief headquarters and foundation of all Allied radio intelligence. The monitoring of the German radio nets and reading of their correspondence made possible the gradual reconstruction of the entire system of German radio communications in the West and, consequently, establishment of the disposition of Wehrmacht commands, higher formations, and units. The British liaison officer, Capt. Kenneth Macfarlane (nicknamed "Pinky" for his rosy complexion), together with the French Capt. Henri Braquenié was in charge of maintaining the connection between Bruno and the equivalent British secret intelligence establishment at Bletchley Park. Macfarlane was in contact with the high command of the British Expeditionary Force in Arras, France, and also had direct teleprinter communication with London and Bletchley Park. He knew all the Bruno secrets, including that of Enigma. Macfarlane's tact, knowledge of the tasks involved and British common sense were particularly valuable in dealing with the egotism and sulkings of the group of disparate people of different nationalities and temperaments who were cooped up, anxious and exhausted.

The main obstacles that the Polish cryptologists had to overcome after reaching France were the changes that the German Chi-Dienst had introduced to Enigma keys on 1 July 1939. Just before the outbreak of war the Poles had broken this new wartime system; on arrival in France, however, they had to reconstruct the entire process as all the relevant documents had been destroyed before they had crossed the border into Rumania. The first Enigma signal to be broken in France did not occur until 28 October. Thereafter, the stream of fresh firsthand information about the Nazi build-up was constantly flowing to the French high command and to London via the Bletchley center.

In fact, the British were building their own cryptological bombe from plans with which Knox and Denniston had become acquainted during their visit to Warsaw before the war. And they were also producing Zygalski's perforated sheets, the only differences being that they used Imperial measures instead of decimals and that they renamed them "Jeffreys' perforated sheets." Their suggestion to open a joint cryptology center in France was rejected by the French, as was the Polish proposal to invite the British cryptographers. Although it was in the time-honored tradition of all secret services not to trust anyone too much, this fact must have been somewhat galling to the British, especially in view of the previous tripartite cooperation. The French interception teams, who worked around the clock, were sending streams of signal traffic by teleprinters to the cryptanalysts, who also worked around the clock to keep up with the incoming volume. They were, however, seriously handicapped by the shortage of Enigma machines. The Poles had brought two with them from Poland, and the French possessed one model that they had received previously from Warsaw. One machine had to be dismantled to facilitate the production of new machines in France, but this project was going slowly. Lieutenant Colonel Langer was greatly worried about that. In December 1939, he went to London and Bletchley Park, where he arranged for closer cooperation between Bruno and the British establishment under the terms of which Bruno was to do the research and Bletchley Park the technical work.

What was the content of the Enigma intercepts read by the Poles at Bruno? Particularly important were Enigma messages that referred to the procedure of the German communications system. Every day before midnight, signals were broadcast, informing all radio stations in a given net about the transmission hours, wavelengths, call-signs, etc., that would be in effect the following day. French monitoring stations used this information to prepare for intercepting Nazi Enigma correspondence the next day. A separate category of Enigma decrypts told of methods used by the Germans to camouflage their orders of battle and radio traffic (*Verschleierung*) and to mislead actively the Allied high commands (*Täuschung*).

In his book on Enigma, Bertrand lists twenty-odd categories of cipher intercepts that were solved and read at Bruno. We shall name only the most characteristic ones, indicative of the range of information available from this source: situation reports (*Morgenmeldung, Tagesmeldung, Tagesabschlussmeldung, Abendmeldung*); reports on intelligence collected by German staff about the Allied forces (*Aufklärungsmeldung*); orders of battle of German higher formations (*Gliederung*); directives for combat readiness (*Alarmbereitschaft*); combat orders (*Einsatzbefehl*); combat reports (*Gefechtsmeldung*); air fleet orders (*Flottenbefehl*); information on logistics (*Nachschub*); and special operations (*Sonderunternehmen*).

In addition to the main department at Bruno concerned with Enigma, a counterespionage section was created whose task was to solve the enciphered reports of German agents and the instructions transmitted to them by Abwehr and SD stations in Germany. This work was handled by two French officers, Captains Marlière and Chapadaux, and by Polish engineer Antoni Palluth. Over a few months, 287 radio transmissions by Nazi agents were read and passed on to counterintelligence, which sought to locate and destroy the spy transmitters.

In the period just preceding the Norwegian campaign, which began on 9 April 1940, numerous Enigma decrypts dealt with the intentions and moves of the German commands. Three days before German troops invaded Denmark and Norway (Operation Weserübung), Bruno read a directive from the Wehrmacht high command from which the direction of the approaching attack could be inferred: Nazi press and radio coverage of these two countries was to be handled in such a way as not to alarm their governments and the Allies prematurely. Also, the forces that were to be used in the invasion were known beforehand.

THE BATTLE OF FRANCE

A few days before the start of the German general offensive against France, a conference of French and British intelligence services took place, presided over by Colonel Gauché, chief of the Deuxième Bureau of the French army. The date of the German attack was predicted accurately, but the participants were unable to establish its strategic goal and main direction. On 10 May 1940, at 5:35 A.M., 136 German divisions, seventeen of them armored or motorized, opened a powerful offensive, trampling over Holland, Luxembourg, and Belgium, and shortly thereafter reaching France.

In the first days of the German attack, part of Bruno's personnel were moved from Gretz-Armainvillers to the Paris Deuxième Bureau headquarters at 2 bis, avenue de Tourville. The Polish cryptologists and their French colleagues did all they could to keep up the normal work routine. That was not easy. Just before opening their general offensive on the tenth, the Germans had changed the procedures for using the Enigmas, across all their armed forces. The modifications proved effective: for the first few days of the campaign, the Allies were unable to look over the shoulders of the Nazi commanders. But this setback did not last long: by the tenth day of war, the Polish cryptologists were once again reading Enigma. According to Bertrand, "it took superhuman, day-and-night effort to overcome this new difficulty: on 20 May, decryptment resumed."

It also proved possible to improve upon the already broad Enigma intelligence that had been available during the Norwegian campaign. In addition to the operational orders, daily situation reports and so on, timely information became available on special operations set in motion by ad hoc decisions by Hitler, Wehrmacht commander in chief Brauchitsch, or Luftwaffe chief Göring. This created unique opportunities for counter operations, but not even the most superb intelligence could by itself have done the trick. During these feverish days, the Polish cryptologists worked around the clock, never leaving the building on avenue de Tourville. After decryptment, Enigma intelligence summaries were prepared for the Allied high command and the staffs of the field armies. As the front disintegrated and other sources of intelligence shrank, Enigma information became increasingly vital. Its accuracy soon came to be appreciated; the "Yellow Pages" printed on thin paper in a score of copies were eagerly snapped up by generals and colonels of the French high command, some of whom waited at the entrance to the cryptologists' room or even spent nights in the building in order to get their hands on the hottest information. But even the best intelligence data could not reinforce the Allied positions or stop massed tanks and airplanes that "Operation Yellow," masterminded by Hitler and his chief strategist, General von Manstein, had pitted against France. German spearheads were going around the Maginot Line from the northwest and were tearing deep into the rear of the Allied armies.

The Polish codebreakers experienced many bitter moments. In return for supplying the Allies with precise information, they expected enemy intentions to be appropriately counteracted. Unfortunately, this was not so. An example of a chance passed up was the French high command's reaction to information about the German High Command organizing—not at all with "lightning" speed, but over a fairly long time and with some hesitation—a massive air raid on Paris. The first facts on the planned operation, "Sonderunternehmen Paula" ("Operation Paula"), were obtained from Enigma on 26 May, and subsequent Nazi orders were followed with the greatest attention. Implementing orders by Luftwaffe commands, detailing plans for the air raid on Paris, with diversionary raids on other targets, were read on 29–30 May (seven messages), 31 May (three messages), and 1 June (five messages). In this way, the Allied command was kept abreast of German preparations for Operation Paula. In spite of that, it took no countermeasures since, according to the commander of the French Air Force, General Vuillemin, "he did not have the hundred fighter aircraft necessary unless he stripped the front of that number." At 3:00 P.M., formations of German bombers appeared over the Greater Paris area. The main targets of the raid were the Renault and Citroën plants, but bombs also fell murderously on residential districts. The French Air Force did nothing.

On 10 June, Italian forces struck at France from the Alps, though they made little headway and only increased the chaos and confusion. Stukas, Heinkels, and Messerschmitts ruled the skies over France as they had done eight months earlier over Poland, and with the same savagery massacred the retreating troops and refugees on the roads. The order also came, on the tenth, to evacuate Bruno. The column of a dozen vehicles set out from Gretz-Armainvillers, heading south. The town of La Fèrte-Saint Aubin was designated as the new operations site. On arrival, the Poles activated their Enigmas and once again read German signals. The decrypts, alas, bore testimony to the enemy's triumph. The next stopover for Bruno was the town of Vensat in the Massif Central. Here again decryptment resumed, but the General Staff was no longer responding. Contact with it was secured on 17 June, but only to receive orders for continued evacuation towards Toulouse. Here, on the twenty-second, the Polish team was informed that Pétain had signed an armistice with the Germans, which really meant capitulation. Two days later, in tremendous haste, Bertrand managed to fly the foreign personnel of Bruno—fifteen Poles and seven Spaniards—in three military planes to Algeria.

After the collapse of France, the Polish codebreaking team continued their quiet struggle against the Nazis. A new period of clandestine operations began. In the terms of the armistice, the Germans stipulated that all radio intelligence facilities were immediately to be turned over to them, together with lists of personnel. A split appeared among the French officers. "Loyalists" rigidly stuck by their oaths and kept faith with Pétain; they believed in his political "good sense," which was expected to save the country from complete catastrophe. Others, including Bertrand, at once took a position decidedly opposed to seeking accommodation with the Nazis. France was reduced to a rump state comprising about two-fifths of her former area. The two million–man French army was reduced to 100,000 men. Close to a million prisoners of war were kept penned up in camps or sent to forced labor in Germany. Even as France was collapsing, on 18 June 1940, General de Gaulle proclaimed the Free French Movement and a continuation of the struggle. But in the occupied north as well as in the unoccupied southern zone, centers of resistance were expiring and apathy had swept over most people.

CADIX IN SOUTHERN FRANCE

Upon arrival in Algeria, the Poles were registered under fictitious names and quartered in Oran, then in Algiers at the Touring Club Hotel. They tried not to attract the attention of the French-Algerian authorities, among whom were many supporters of accommodation with Germany. Meanwhile, ever-larger Nazi units were arriving in North Africa. Apart from outposts of the German branch of the Armistice Commission, the Abwehr and SD were setting up their own networks of agents.

As early as mid-July 1940, Colonel Bertrand presented his superiors with a proposal for clandestine resumption of radio intelligence. Such operations could proceed only in deep secrecy, since in the event of exposure the Nazis would accuse the Vichy authorities of violating the terms of the armistice, with incalculable consequences. Gen. Juliusz Kleeberg, the semi-official representative in southern France of the Polish government-in-exile, concluded, in consultation with London, that the Polish cryptologists could render valuable services to the Allies and that they would do best by continuing to work clandestinly in France, right under the enemy's nose. While working together with the French, they would be subordinate to the Polish commander in chief's General Staff in Britain, and would receive the code name "Ekspozytura 300" ("Field Office 300").

The Franco-Polish plan was, thus, to resume offensive radio intelligence on the territory of unoccupied France, using Nazi wireless dispatches intercepted by patriotic officers at the Vichy monitoring system (Groupement des Contrôles Radioélectriques de L'Intérieurs, or GCR). The clandestine codebreaking center would also solve German enciphered messages supplied by members of the resistance movement in the French postal system. It was necessary, however, to act quickly, since Nazi intelligence services and the Gestapo were wrapping southern France ever more tightly in their tentacles. A favorable circumstance, on the other hand, was the fact that, in July–August 1940, the Germans' attention was absorbed by the great air battle of Britain and preparations to invade the British Isles.

Bertrand, now alias "Monsieur Barsac," was meanwhile preparing new facilities for a clandestine decryptment center in southern France. The Château des Fouzes was finally selected as the site, near the historic little town of Uzès (population *ca.* 4,000) and not far from Nimes and Marseilles. By virtue of a special authorization from the French SR (intelligence service), "Monsieur Barsac" purchased the château, all the necessary false papers drawn up to avoid suspicion.

During September 1940, the Poles, who had evacuated to North Africa, received documents issued in fictitious names and then, in twos and threes, returned to southern France. Chief cryptologist Rejewski was now "Pierre Renaud," a "*lycée* professor from Nantes," Zygalski was "René Sergent," Langer was "Charles Lange," and Palluth was "Jean Lenoir." Those who did not speak fluent French had been supplied with credible biographies as naturalized foreigners—businessmen, craftsmen, etc. It never occurred to the Germans that the defeated French would continue transmitting radio intelligence in the face of the ban expressly forbidding the French to engage in any intelligence operations.

In early October 1940, three and a half months after the rout of the French army and the disbanding of the Bruno center, a reactivated radio intelligence station, code-named "Cadix," resumed operations. The new Cadix center consisted of the following units: the Polish cryptological team (fifteen persons), the Spanish team (seven persons), and the French staff (nine persons, including Bertrand and his wife, Mary), making a total of thirty-two persons. The cryptologists set to work using three cipher machines that they had managed to save, as well as monitoring equipment and radio transmitters. Four more copies of Enigma were made from parts ordered at the beginning of 1940. The Polish team, though in some way subordinate to the center's French management, communicated by radio directly with the staff of the Polish commander in chief in London, receiving assignments and sending in periodic reports, sometimes, it is said, communicating via Enigma and ending the message with an ironic "Heil Hitler!"

Decryptment began as soon as Cadix had been organized and took in the following kinds of monitored materials:

- signals of Wehrmacht staffs and units stationed in France, Germany, and territories occupied by or dominated by the Nazis: in Belgium, Bulgaria, Czechoslovakia, Hungary, Libya, Poland, the USSR, Yugoslavia, and elsewhere;

- signals of SS and police in Austria, Czechoslovakia, France, Holland, Luxembourg, Norway, Poland, and in occupied parts of the USSR;

- radio correspondence of Abwehr and SD agents in France and in North Africa with their intelligence headquarters in Germany;

- radio correspondence of the German Armistice Commission headquarters at Wiesbaden with its stations in southern France and North Africa, and among its field stations.

After the German invasion of the Soviet Union on 22 June 1941, the main theater of the war shifted away from France. Cadix's monitoring took in the Russian front only at night, but on the other hand messages were easily picked up from German territory and from various occupied countries. SS and Wehrmacht radios in France transmitted many reports that gave information on the growing resistance movement. Decryptment of these reports enabled Cadix to warn clandestine organizations of impending punitive expeditions and sweeps; even individual persons were warned that the Nazi police sought them. In September 1941, a cipher was broken that turned out to be actively in use for communications between a group of German secret agents operating in French Mediterranean ports and the Abwehr headquarters in Stuttgart. The reconstructed spy reports were sent to Marseilles, where the counterintelligence branch of the Resistance discovered the transmitter and neutralized the agents.

Vichy France was under a constant threat of a Nazi occupation of the whole of France. The Cadix center was in constant danger of being discovered or denounced and had to observe strict precautions. Security dictated that individuals at Cadix should know only what was indispensable to their work. They were functionally isolated, so that the enciphering officers and the radio operators knew nothing of what the mathematician cryptologists did in their rooms, the doors of which were closed and the windows barred.

In spite of difficulties, nearly all the Poles at Cadix established contact by letters with their families in Poland by way of other countries and safe people, with the help of their French comrades who found safe cover addresses for them. For example, Rejewski's wife received a letter from a nun in Switzerland informing her that her husband was in southern France and, later, a postcard from Spain with greetings from him in Spanish. Her guess that her husband was in Spain was incorrect, but at least she knew he was alive. Relations among the Polish team were not always perfect; occasional conflict was inevitable among the confined men who were in constant danger of a surprise raid by the Vichy police. At the same time, the hardships endured by the men cemented the group together. They survived by maintaining mental and physical fitness. They were permitted short rides on bicycle to the nearest town of Uzès, but no contact with the local population. Their days were spent working long hours and, in their free time, amusing themselves with singing contests, celebrating every possible holiday, national and personal, and frog hunting, a pastime in the French gastronomical tradition.

In early 1941, an overseas station of the Polish-French Cadix radio intelligence center had been set up in North Africa. The outpost, code-named "P.O.1 Kouba," was located on the outskirts of the city of Algiers, and was headed by Major Maksymilian Ciężki. He commanded a team of six to eight codebreakers and radio operators, who rotated back to southern France every three or four months. Kouba, apart from its main task, which included the interception and decoding of German and Italian signals, was also responsible for ensuring radio communication between the Allied intelligence network, "Rygor," led by Maj. (later Gen.) Mieczysław Z. Słowikowski, and the Allied headquarters in London. Many secret reports from the Rygor organization, whose task was to collect intelligence for the planning of the Anglo-American landings in North Africa (code-named "Torch"), were transmitted to Britain via Uzès in southern France. A Polish "Lacida" cipher machine produced by the AVA factory before the war was used for this purpose.

For his great contribution to the successful landing operation in North Africa, in November 1942, Słowikowski received the American Order of Merit and the Order of the British Empire.

One rotational exchange of Polish codebreakers across the Mediterranean ended tragically; the French ship SS *Lamoricière,* on which the Polish team was returning from Algiers to France, hit a reef or mine and sank on 9 January 1942. Jerzy Różycki, Jan Graliński, and Piotr Smoleński lost their lives in the catastrophe, as did a French intelligence officer, Capt. François Lane, who had accompanied them.

In the summer of 1942, signs of danger to the clandestine radio intelligence center at Uzès began to appear. Cadix was receiving reports on the concentration of German troops at the demarcation line separating the occupied northern France from the southern "Free Zone." In late September, a special German signal counterintelligence unit (*Funkabwehr*) arrived in southern France, and soon began to feel its way around. There were signs that the German detector unit was on the trail of the Cadix radio station, but Bertrand soon learned at the prefecture in neaby Nimes of the arrival of this unit and warned Uzès. One day Rejewski, looking out of the window, noticed a Vichy police truck of the mobile direction-finding team, recognizable by the vehicle's protruding circular antenna. It was approaching and within sight of the château. But by some extraordinarily good luck, the radio station was not its destination.

On 8 November 1942, the Allies landed in North Africa. Three days later, the Nazis abruptly invaded the "Free Zone," but by the ninth Cadix had already been completely evacuated, disappearing from the region of Uzès. The Cadix personnel was instructed to proceed south to the coast for embarkation. Over their two years at Cadix, the Polish cryptologists had deciphered a total of 4,679 German secret dispatches. Since nearly all the signals comprised two parts transmitted in separate sessions, Cadix's whole effort netted about nine thousand deciphered messages sent by the Wehrmacht, SS, Gestapo, and other agencies of the Third Reich.

Following the German occupation of southern France, on personal orders of the Führer and with the cooperation of senior French officers, mass arrests by the Gestapo of Allied intelligence personnel began. Fortunately, the existence of Cadix was a well-kept secret and not even the ciphers department of the French post-Armistice army knew about it.

The members of the Cadix group again scattered in different directions, but the Poles of Ekspozytura 300 were better prepared this time. They resolved to try to escape to Britain via Spain and Portugal. [In describing the final days in France of his Polish colleagues, Bertrand said: *"Quelle aubaine pour les Anglais!"* ("What a windfall for the English!")] The Cadix group split up by twos and threes. The organizers showed great ingenuity in their methods of escape. Some members of the group, with the help of Resistance networks, were taken as handcuffed "prisoners" from the Franco-Spanish border by train to Portugal, where they were admitted as refugees. Some traveled as stowaways on passenger ships from Marseilles bound for North Africa, others on fishing boats or private craft, still others escaped across the Pyrenees, and some of them fell into traps set up by smugglers or border guards who turned them in to the Germans for rewards. The Polish group selected false identities for themselves and disguised themselves as suited their appearance, knowledge of languages, and education, so as to best escape detection by roaming German or Italian security agents. The dark-complexioned of them could pass as Hungarians, who were allied with Germany; others who had good knowledge of languages could pass themselves off as French, Swiss, or German. When they reached the Côte d'Azur, which was in the Italian occupation zone, they wandered between Nice, Cannes, Marseilles, and Toulouse, with some narrow escapes. When things began to get too hot there, Rejewski and Zygalski, with the help of Resistance agents, reached Perpignan in the Pyrenees. From there, avoiding German and Vichy patrols and with the help of a smuggler, the two marched over uninhabited, rough mountain terrain to reach the Spanish border. The Spanish side of the Pyrenees swarmed with agents of Franco's security police and even before the two reached the border in January 1943, they were arrested and imprisoned in Merida.

The same fate awaited a large number of other refugees of various nationalities fleeing France. Some Poles landed in Franco's concentration camps, of which there were several, such as Modelo, Las Misiones, and Miranda, together with several hundred other foreign prisoners. In Barcelona, on the way to Las Misiones camp, they were escorted by guards and paraded down the streets of the city, manacled, before gaping onlookers. Although Spanish camps cannot be compared with German concentration camps, brutal beatings and a starvation diet were the order of the day. The Polish prisoners, in an effort to escape the camp and rejoin their fighting units, used ingenious tricks. Under the guise of joining the camp choir, a few Polish soldiers dug an underground tunnel over a few weeks from the chapel to the outside wall and escaped. Several of the Cadix officers imprisoned in the Miranda camp expressed a desire to enter a monastery; after an appeal to the Papal Nuncio in Madrid, they took monastic vows and, as so-called monks, were able to make their way to Britain via Portugal. The Polish prisoners in the Spanish camps were allowed contacts with the Polish Red Cross in Barcelona who, taking advantage of the ignorance of the Polish language by the Spanish guards, sent messages to the detainees in the guise of a list of names of Polish prisoners who were to receive food packages:

1. Zygmunt Przybylski

2. Komisja Przyjezdza (Commission Arrives)

3. Jutro Zestolicy (Tomorrowfrom Thecapital)

4. Bedzie Uwas (Itwill Visityou)

5. Przygotowujcie Uwagi (Prepare Remarks)

6. Owarunkach Wobozie (Onconditions Incamp)

7. Ispis Chorych (And Sicklist)

8. Trzymaj Ciesie (Good Luck)

9. Mikolaj Cieslak

10. Marian Wozniak

The Polish prisoners enjoyed responding to the morning roll call when the commandant of the camp lifted his hand and shouted: "España!" to which they were expected to call back in unison: "Granda!" The Poles happily responded with a full-throated "Granda!" because, in vernacular Polish, *granda* means "scandal" or "racket." The Spaniards must have thought that they had convinced the Poles to support Franco.

Rejewski and Zygalski, on being released from prison after two months, were placed under the protection of the Polish Red Cross and reached Portugal in the summer of that year. From there they traveled on a British destroyer to Gibraltar and then by plane to England, where they arrived in July 1943.

Lieutenant Colonel Langer and Major Ciężki were not so lucky for, on crossing the French frontier in March 1943, they were betrayed by their guides and captured by the Germans. They were first held in Stalag 122 in Compiègne, then taken to SS concentration camp #4 at Schloss Eisenberg in Czechoslovakia, which they endured for two years. After their capture, it took the Germans six months to realize whom they held.

In March 1944, Langer appeared before a joint Gestapo-Wehrmacht commission and was asked to become a double agent for them. One of the questions put to him was whether Enigma had been decrypted by the Polish Cipher Bureau before the war and later in France. Langer took a big risk. He admitted that the Poles had solved the Enigma before the war. However, he said, the coding changes made by the Germans in 1938 had made it impossible for the Poles to continue reading the Enigma after the start of the war. Since he was not a cipher expert, he suggested that his interrogators confirm with Ciężki what he said. To his great relief, Ciężki repeated what Langer had said. The Germans believed them, convinced by now that the newly doctored and constantly improved Enigma was indeed invincible. This answer saved the Allied codebreaking operation at a crucial time, just before D-Day. Later, Langer and Ciężki were either released by the Germans or "liberated" by the advancing Allied forces.

Also captured by the Germans were Palluth and Fokczynski. They were sent to the Nazi concentration camp Sachsenhausen-Oranienburg, near Berlin. Palluth was killed during an Allied air raid; Fokczynski died from exhaustion.

Bertrand was captured by the Germans in Paris on 5 January 1944. The Abwehr told him that they knew who he was and asked him to switch sides. Bertrand pretended to agree, was released and fled with his wife. With the help of the British, he was flown to England on 2 June 1944.

Rejewski and Zygalski, on their arrival in England in 1943, perhaps contrary to their expectations because they knew that cryptanalysts were badly needed, were not allowed even to approach Bletchley Park, the most secret place in Britain. They were assigned to the Radio Battalion of the Polish commander in chief at Stanmore-Boxmoor, near London, headed by Maj. Tadeusz Lisicki. The unit, which maintained radio communication with all Polish armed forces of the Western theater of war, included also a radio intelligence branch, headed by Captain Kazimierz Zielinski. The two brilliant Polish cryptologists occupied themselves mainly with breaking SS and SD codes and ciphers. Every early reading of a directive or order from SS or SD headquarters could save the lives of Allied soldiers or members of the anti-Nazi Resistance. Under the strict rules of security, their two-year stay in occupied France under German control, followed by several months in a Spanish jail, had tainted them in the eyes of the British and made them ineligible for employment at Bletchley Park—or at least that is how it was presented to them! The reason for waning British interest in the Polish cryptographers may have been that some of those at Bletchley Park who had been connected with Enigma before the war and who had attended the meetings at Warsaw and Pyry, were now gone. Denniston had been replaced in 1942, and Knox had died in 1943.

With regard to the mistrust by the British of their one-time benefactors we now know in hindsight that the British "old boy" method of recruitment was a miserable failure as evidenced by the unsuspected presence in their midst of such traitors as Kim Philby, Guy Burgess, Donald Maclean, and Anthony Blunt. Another such traitor was John Cairncross, the Soviet mole who gave raw German Enigma data to the KGB. It consisted of precise information on Luftwaffe with details of the strength, unit numbers, and location of the Luftwaffe squadrons. The same information was provided for the Wehrmacht—a clear picture of the order of battle of German land and air forces. Cairncross boasts in his book, *The Enigma Story,* that he helped the Russians win the famous tank battle of Kursk. He had no qualms about his treachery, although the dissemination of Enigma intelligence was absolutely forbidden, even among Allies, since the British did not completely trust the security of Russian intelligence. In retrospect, it is ironic that with such treachery in their midst, the British should have mistrusted the Poles, their most loyal and faithful allies.

In this connection, David Kahn wrote in his book, *Seizing the Enigma*: "The cryptanalysts who escaped reached England in 1943 after harrowing trips. The Poles reaped the customary reward of the innovators whose efforts have benefited others: exclusion. The British kept Rejewski and others from any work on Enigma, assigning them instead to a signals company of the Polish forces in exile, where they solved low-level ciphers. It was not one of Britain's finest hours!"

Maybe it was just another example of the N.I.H. ("not invented here," therefore of no value) syndrome—an attitude common in scientific establishments and labs in Britain. But it does seem suspect in this context. There must have been a good deal of professional envy among the British cryptanalysts who wanted to keep all the credit for themselves.

Enigma in Great Britain: Ultra

The British agency called the Government Code and Cipher School (GCCS) was responsible for all government-ciphering activities and was a branch of the Foreign Office. Just before the start of the war, it was moved from London to Bletchley Park, an estate in the town of Bletchley, some fifty miles northwest of London, about halfway between Cambridge and Oxford. The GCCS cryptanalysts were mostly recruited from those two universities. They were of varied backgrounds but most of them were mathematicians, physicists, linguists, historians, or classical scholars, all intellectually inclined and highly educated.

Secure radio communication and decryptment of enemy codes and ciphers were of exceptional importance to Britain. The reason was simple: Britain's defense depended primarily on her Navy and Air Force; and in these, communications and thus the entire command system were based on radio and cryptography. Conversely, intelligence, for the British, chiefly meant maintaining first-rate interception and code-breaking methods to permit their constant surveillance of German, but also Italian, naval and air fleets. In wartime, listening in on such communications became a matter of survival, of getting an edge on an enemy who could deal the British Isles a mortal blow only from the sea or the air. Hence, the uncommon doggedness with which the British attacked enemy codes and ciphers in the First, and still more in the Second World War.

It is now known—although British sources remain scanty—that, beginning in the mid-1930s, GCCS had worked hard at breaking the Nazi Enigma machine cipher but had failed to make headway. Alfred Dillwyn Knox did manage, most likely in 1938, to break the cipher of General Franco's army, based on the commercial model of Enigma. But the latter bore about the same relation to Hitler's military Enigma as did the Spanish rebel forces to German military might. Thus the ciphers of the Wehrmacht, SS, and other key agencies of the Third Reich remained for the British experts through all these years a tantalizing riddle.

The British received from the Poles a fairly good introduction to the Enigma system. The decrypting and dissemination of intercepted Enigma messages at Bletchley was called "Ultra." The best use of Ultra was in conveying strategic (long-range plans) rather than tactical (immediate, under battle conditions) information, for example, in North Africa when Enigma decrypts revealed information regarding supply convoys to Rommel.

Concerning the date when reading the German Enigma code was first mastered in Britain, initially with the aid of Polish equipment (the Polish Enigma replica, the cryptological bombe, Zygalski's perforated sheets, etc.), there are discrepancies among the sources. F. W. Winterbotham writes that the first German Air Force ciphers were read in their entirety at the end of February 1940. Polish and French sources, however, indicate that the British had been actively collaborating with Bruno, the Polish-French decryptment center, since at least December 1939, exchanging solved Enigma keys daily by teletype. Polish wartime accounts on Enigma include a report by Lt. Col. Gwido Langer giving dates of keys solved from January to June 1940 and stating that, of the total of 126 Nazi Enigma keys cracked during this period, 83 percent were solved with British participation. "When I was in England in December 1939," writes Langer in another surviving document, "the British asked that our specialists be turned over to them. At that time I personally took the position that we must remain in France where our armed forces were being formed. The French rejected the British proposal to create a common unit at Bruno. The upshot was that we were to conduct the research, and the British to do the technical and day-to-day work."

Such was the Allied order of battle in the struggle with Enigma in the first months of the war. The Poles still led in basic research and theoretical work. The French, at that time the strongest partner of the alliance in terms of land forces, guarded their primacy in intelligence concerning the German armed forces preparing for the offensive. As for the British, most of their brilliant achievements in decryptment came in the latter part of the war. Nevertheless, from the autumn of 1939 until May 1940, while the "phoney war" was being waged, actually only by the intelligence services on the two sides, considerable progress was made at Bletchley toward mastering the techniques for the regular solving of Enigma.

Like the Enigma operations in Poland and France before it, British Ultra involved three functions: (1) interception, (2) decryptment, and (3) translation, followed by assessment and distribution of the information, suitably edited so as to protect the Enigma secret.

The usefulness of intelligence material depends on its timely dissemination; therefore an extensive net of Special Liaison Units (SLU) was created that eventually spanned nearly all the continents of the globe. The man responsible was then-Squadron Leader F. W. Winterbotham, who originally set up an SIS intelligence team at Bletchley on behalf of the Air Force. Having learned of Enigma's potential, he devised a plan, approved by Colonel Menzies, for the fastest and most secret distribution of the intercepted material to the field. A central coordinating department for all three services was then established. This was a great improvement as, until then, the three services had acted independently, with inevitable duplication of effort. At first, there was some difficulty in implementing the plan, as the three services (especially the Navy) were reluctant to share information, but eventually they all agreed to cooperate and set themselves up in Hut 3.

The task of the SLUs was to convey the substance of decrypted enemy radio messages to the Allied high commands in Great Britain, continental Europe, Africa, Asia, and Australia. All British SLU members were Air Force intelligence and signals personnel and wore RAF uniforms. Each Special Liaison Unit comprised an officer and a small section of cipher sergeants and radio operators. The SLU brought the message to the commander of the group to which it was attached, without telling him how the information was obtained. Absolute secrecy was kept, then the message was personally destroyed after the commanding officer had read it. Some commanders and senior personnel did not like acting upon messages whose origin the SLU could not give them, but with tact they could be convinced to comply. It was at this stage that the intelligence chiefs of all three services agreed to call this Enigma source "Ultra" to distinguish it from other intelligence nets. Some high military commanders liked to have their SLUs physically as close as possible, sometimes within fifty yards from their tents; others, such as General Montgomery, would banish them to a solitary spot half a mile away, allegedly for fear of the enemy getting a bearing on their radio transmitters. SLU chiefs were authorized to intervene if they felt that a planned operation might give away the Ultra/ Enigma secret. The work of the Special Liaison Units organization was facilitated by the support it was given personally by Winston Churchill, who himself often took a SLU along on his numerous wartime inspection tours.

The mainstream of German army radio intercepts, after the collapse of France, flowed in to Bletchley from a station at Chatham, about thirty miles east of London, near the mouth of the Thames. German Luftwaffe signals were intercepted mainly by stations at Cheadle and Chicksands Priory, in Bedfordshire. German Navy intercepts came in from Flowersdown and Scarborough, on the eastern coast.

The internal cryptology system at Bletchley reflected that of the enemy whose decrypts were read, each enemy service using a different system according to its particular needs. Thus, the naval section dealt with foreign naval intercepts; other sections worked on foreign army, air force, and diplomatic intercepts. At Bletchley, the military and naval sections each evolved into two parts: cryptanalysis, which broke the cryptograms; and intelligence, which extracted information from the solved intercepts.

As Bletchley grew, a number of temporary huts were added to provide working space for the increasing population: Hut 8 housed naval cryptanalysts, Hut 4 naval intelligence analysts who translated and commented on the solved intercepts; similarly, Hut 3 decrypted German army and air force messages, and Hut 6 provided analyses for these solutions.

In the years 1940–45, the Bletchley radio intelligence center had expanded both territorially and in terms of personnel, employing first hundreds and by the end of the war approximately nine thousand military and civilian personnel—codebreakers, intelligence analysts, interpreters, technicians, etc., including some two thousand WRENs and WAAFs operating communication and cryptographic equipment. Before the advent of Enigma, they were engaged in breaking non-machine cipher systems in the diverse areas of foreign, diplomatic, and military traffic; but once Enigma was adopted, all three German services started using this enciphering machine in its different forms. By the middle of the war there were a dozen different naval Enigma nets—one for surface ships in the North Sea and the Atlantic, another for U-boats, a third for Mediterranean surface ships, another for Mediterranean U-boats, and so on.

PRINCIPAL PERSONALITIES AT BLETCHLEY PARK

During World War I, the naval codebreaking section, Room 40, was part of the British Admiralty. The section was later transferred to the Foreign Office, expanded into the Government Code and Cipher School, and moved to Bletchley Park. Cmdr. Alastair Denniston, who had been one of the cryptographers at the British Admiralty, became the head of Bletchley, serving in that position in the first part of the war. In February 1942, he was replaced, due to ill health, by his second in command, Comdr. Edward Travis, who ran Bletchley until the end of the war. Cambridge graduates Alfred Dillwyn Knox, in charge of work on the German Enigma cipher machine, Alan Turing, Gordon Welchman, and John Jeffreys were among the principal characters in the Ultra story as it developed at Bletchley. The number of Cambridge professors of mathematics and their students, naturally enough, proliferated at Bletchley as each one tried to recruit his own brightest students.

Knox was a brilliant scholar with wide interests. While at Eton he had already shown a remarkable mathematical talent, and at Cambridge he drew attention by the variety of his interests and his madcap originality. He combined a sharp intellect with remarkable absent-mindedness. He was comically inept at mechanical things, such as when he twice severely injured himself driving a motor vehicle or when he burned himself badly with an acetylene lamp. He was essentially an idea man. His great powers of intuition brought him good results, such as in 1917 when, while lying in his bath (in the manner of Archimedes), he hit on the code used by the German Navy to give orders to their U-boat fleet (as discussed in *Intercept* by Józef Garliński). He was intolerant of people who could not understand him and he disliked the routine at Bletchley, which was inevitably monotonous.

Alan Turing was another gifted and eccentric cryptologist at Bletchley. He began to work at Bletchley in September 1939 as a young man in his late twenties. Very soon thereafter, he demonstrated his exceptional electro-mechanical talents when he built a device eventually named the "Turing bombe." Although it was largely based on its Polish prototype, the *bomba* (of which he received the plans in December 1939 from Polish experts who had come from France on a short visit to Bletchley especially for that purpose), he laid out the entire theoretical framework for tackling the Enigma in all its variations. Some say that this feat surpassed Rejewski's earlier achievement. Like Knox, Turing was a mathematical genius, painfully shy and extremely absentminded. He let his hair grow long and wore strangely cut, crumpled clothes. It is said that during the war he feared that the value of the pound would drop, so he collected a large amount of silver coins, melted them down, and hid them in the grounds of Bletchley Park. Unfortunately after the war ended, the great mathematical mind was unable to remember where he buried it. As early as 1936 he presented a paper on the construction of the first artificial brain, the earliest computer. He had no difficulty understanding the Polish bombes, and he was the first designer of the British bombes.

Gordon Welchman, a lecturer in mathematics and a fellow of Sidney Sussex College at Cambridge, specialized in the algebraic geometry of multidimensional space. He was recruited in 1938 and engaged in codebreaking and setting up the system at Bletchley. A gifted mathematician, but also an organization man, unlike Knox, he helped to transform Bletchley, in the fall of 1939, into a smoothly running, well-coordinated organization with a large staff dealing with the deciphering and dissemination of a huge number of intercepts. Welchman cooperated with Turing in improving the Polish bombe. The British machine was made up of twelve Enigmas joined together so that five of their new bombes represented all sixty rotor possibilities—the solution of which was the Poles' biggest problem in late 1939. Welchman wrote at length about Enigma and the different personalities involved in his book, *The Hut Six Story.*

Another mathematician at Bletchley was the brilliant young John Jeffreys, also a former lecturer at Cambridge who worked closely with Welchman. He worked principally on improving Zygalski's perforated sheets, henceforth referred to as "Jeffreys' sheets" (1,560 perforations to allow for sixty combinations of the five-rotor Enigma). These were mechanically punched by the team at Bletchley, and sixty sets were sent to France to their counterparts at Bruno. The British had infinitely greater technical resources as well as more money and personnel than did the Poles before the war. It may be remembered that the Poles, lacking personnel, had to cut these sheets manually and had only succeeded in preparing two sets of twenty-six combinations before the war broke out—an insignificant amount!

Reading Abwehr's Enigma messages that had been unraveled by Knox provided advance warning of attempts by German intelligence to infiltrate agents into Britain. In the early years of the war, the British had successfully caught and "turned" German spies operating in Britain and, through them, fed false information to the Germans. This fact was confirmed in the exchanges among the different Abwehr stations using Enigma ciphers. In this way, in the spring and summer of 1941, a number of agents smuggled in from Norway as refugees were arrested as soon as they set foot on British soil.

One of the most brilliant deceptions of the war, described in Ewan Montagu's book, *The Man Who Never Was,* was to float from a British submarine a dead man, supposedly a Royal Marine officer, on whose body were planted documents suggesting that the Allied invasion would take place in Sardinia and Greece, instead of in Sicily. The body was fished out of the sea on the Spanish coast and, as expected, the information passed on to the Germans. Confirmation of the success of the British deception came from Abwehr's Enigma messages showing that the Germans, on the basis of this false information, had moved some of their forces from Sicily to Sardinia and the Balkans, thus greatly relieving pressure on the Allied invasion forces.

THE IMPACT OF ENIGMA/ULTRA ON ALLIED STRATEGY AND MILITARY OPERATIONS

As far as the first phase of Enigma history is concerned, we have shown that the solution of the German machine cipher and the development of methods offering the permanent possibility of reading them were Polish achievements.

The mathematical methods, Polish Enigma replicas, and the ancillary technology, which were passed on to Bletchley in 1939, enabled the British to exploit and expand these achievements in scale of operations to keep pace with the requirements of the war. While we are able to present the first period of the Enigma operation on the basis of comprehensive Polish sources, information on the use made of the Enigma deciphering, its impact on Allied strategy, and warfare during the Second World War, was largely obtained elsewhere.

Apart from Gustave Bertrand's book (1973), which first broke the silence in the matter, information is mainly to be found in British publications, the most important being those of F. W. (Frederick William) Winterbotham (1974), Patrick Beesly (1977), Ronald Lewin (1978), R. V. (Reginald Victor) Jones (1978), Ralph Bennett (1979), Francis H. Hinsley (1979), Peter Calvocoressi (1980), and Gordon Welchman (1982), as well as numerous periodicals and academic journals. Although only some of the wartime Ultra documents have been made public, enough is already known to give a general idea of the role of Enigma decrypts in various periods and theaters of the Second World War. Since nearly a score of significant books on this subject have already been published, we may confine ourselves to a concise presentation of some of the most characteristic examples.

THE BATTLE OF BRITAIN, 1940

Information provided by Ultra was decisive in winning the Battle of Britain. At the beginning of the war, the Germans had very poor intelligence on the subject of the RAF's fighter strength (in July 1940 they underestimated it by one-third). They knew little of the British capacity for production and rapid repair of aircraft, and they knew nothing about radar. There was similar ignorance on the part of the British with regard to the Luftwaffe. The British placed their hope in Ultra due to the difficulties they had experienced in planting spies on the continent.

The Battle of Britain started in July 1940, when the Luftwaffe attacked shipping and inland targets in England. In August, Air Chief Marshal Sir Hugh Dowding was connected by teleprinter line directly to the SLU's Fighter Command Operations Room at Bletchley. This provided Dowding with information on the strength, location, and readiness for action of individual Luftwaffe units, in advance of coming raids. After 15 September, the number of raids decreased and the Battle of Britain was considered won, with the considerable participation of Polish fighter pilots.

Already back in July, Bletchley was decrypting prolific Enigma radio correspondence from the Luftwaffe command, giving detailed information on the deployment and strength of German air fleets (*Luftflotten*) 2, 3, and 5, which were preparing for massed raids against Britain. On 1 August, Göring ordered the Luftwaffe to defeat the Royal Air Force as soon as possible. Thanks to Enigma decrypts, the British Fighter Command learned the general strategic outlines of the coming air offensive. Göring had assigned zones to his several air fleets, which were to concentrate their bombing raids on British military airfields. In these early days of August, writes F. W. Winterbotham, "the number of German signals began to boil over," and Bletchley received two to three hundred a day to decipher. The large number of Luftwaffe signals exchanged each day among different German units made it easier for Bletchley to decipher them because, as mentioned before, the more signals there are in the same key, the easier it is for cryptologists to read them. On 8 August, Göring issued his order of the day, Operation Adler ("Eagle"). The RAF should be, in Goring's words, "swept from the skies." In less than an hour, the decrypted order was in the hands of Winston Churchill, the Chiefs of Staff, and Air Marshal Hugh Dowding, head of Fighter Command. After the start of the German air offensive, Dowding was regularly provided with sufficient Luftwaffe Enigma decrypts, with precise warning of the timing and objectives of its attacks.

In the early years of the war, the Germans developed a system of intersecting navigational radio beams that helped their bombers locate a large target, such as London. A German transmitting station sent two narrow radio beams (*"Knickebein"*—"crooked leg") along and between which their bombers could travel. Another beam from another station intercepted them over the target. A young British scientist, R. V. Jones, discovered how the system worked in practice, but he did not know the location of the transmitting stations in Germany until an Enigma decrypt revealed it in June 1940. Countermeasures could then be taken.

The rapid growth of demand for intercepts and decrypting made for shortages of personnel at Bletchley. In desperation, Gordon Welchman wrote a letter on 21 October 1941, in which he gave an account of the situation and himself took it directly to Prime Minister Churchill, violating the chain of command. Churchill's response was rapid and positive. The number of personnel was immediately increased. Since Enigma reached into the secret decision-making of the highest German commands, it provided both strategic and tactical information, whereas radar stations, while also valuable, supplied only short-term warning. The Battle of Britain was won by valiant British and Allied fighter pilots, including many Poles, but a significant role in the victory over the Luftwaffe was played by Enigma and Ultra.

NORTH AFRICA AND THE MEDITERRANEAN

All Allied commanders of highest rank in the African campaign of 1941–43, namely, Generals Wavell, Auchinleck, Alexander, and Montgomery, regularly received from Bletchley, through the Special Liaison Units, vital Enigma information on Rommel's Afrika Korps and Italian forces. For example, when Churchill stopped in Egypt on his way back from Moscow, the British high command was able to show him the complete order of battle of Rommel's forces, as well as a dispatch from Rommel to Hitler on 31 August 1942, describing his proposed assault on the British Eighth Army. With this Enigma information, Montgomery had ample time to prepare his countermeasures and to upset the German plans.

The army and the navy of Mussolini's Italy were using the same early Enigma model with which the Italian intervention forces in the Civil War in Spain in 1936–39 had been supplied. Both Italian and German Enigma dispatches from the Mediterranean area were continuously intercepted and read by the Bletchley codebreakers. In late March 1941, the Italian Naval Command (Supermarina) decided to launch a grand offensive against the Allied convoys. On the night of 26–27 March, an assault formation, including one battleship (*Vittorio Veneto*), eight cruisers and thirteen destroyers, was sent into the Aegean Sea. One day earlier, however, the Italian plan had become known to Admiral Cunningham, the British naval commander in Alexandria, thanks to the Ultra decrypt he had received. His task force—three battleships, one aircraft carrier, and nine destroyers—left Alexandria and caught the Italian fleet by surprise. In the naval battles of Gaudo and Matapan, the British fleet sank three cruisers and two destroyers, losing only one aircraft. The Italian assault formation was defeated: the Supermarina lost its strategic initiative and did not undertake any more offensive operations.

The breaking by Bletchley of the German Navy's Mediterranean Enigma key "Porpoise," as well as the previously solved Italian Enigma decrypts, led to the detection of the Axis Mediterranean supply lines and convoy routes in July 1942. Inexplicably, as late as 1944, the Kriegsmarine was still using in the Mediterranean theater of operations the insecure twice-enciphered indicators first discovered by Rejewski in 1938, even though by then the German Navy was using a four-rotor machine in other areas. As a consequence, the RAF and the Royal Navy were able to attack Axis convoys selectively and with precision, because they frequently knew the exact composition of nearly every convoy, including ships' names and what they carried. Enigma reports were directly responsible for sinking at least eighty-six German and Italian supply vessels sailing in armed convoys from Italy to North African ports. This number constitutes about 40 percent of all losses in sea transport suffered by the Axis powers in the Mediterranean.

THE ITALIAN CAMPAIGN

The Enigma radio messages from Hitler's "Wolf's Lair" in eastern Prussia to the German commander in chief in southern Europe, Field Marshal Kesselring, and from his Italian headquarters in Naples to Rommel's Afrika Korps, were intercepted and read at Bletchley with amazing regularity. Allied landing operations and the Italian campaign beginning with Operation Husky, the invasion of Sicily, were largely based on Enigma information. Before the start of the Italian campaign, the Special Liaison Unit at La Marsa, near Carthage, was handling two hundred Enigma dispatches every twenty-four hours. The invasion of Sicily triggered the collapse of Mussolini's regime in Italy in the summer of 1943. During the whole Italian campaign of 1943–44, Ultra gave the Allies outstanding intelligence on the enemy's strength, location, and intentions. Bletchley's cryptological work during the Second World War was largely facilitated by Hitler, who was constantly using Enigma radio signals for intervening in many military decisions at lower echelons of command. "I'd like to thank him," remarked ironically the British Chief of the Imperial Staff, Alan Brooke, after the war. "He was worth forty divisions for us!"

THE BATTLE OF THE ATLANTIC

As of 1980, Britain's archives held, for the period from mid-1941 to late 1944 alone, about 324,000 decrypted Enigma messages dealing with the war at sea. Day and night, Bletchley sent to the Admiralty's Operational Intelligence Center (OIC) in London an average of eleven decrypts an hour. The duel between the British OIC and its German opponent, the B-Dienst, had many dramatic turning points.

The first successes with solving naval Enigmas came in 1941, but they did not occur on a regular basis. The Luftwaffe Enigma signals, which were read from late spring 1940, were easier to break because there was a larger number of them sent each day, which revealed certain patterns, and because its operators were sloppy. As the discipline among German army encoders was better, Bletchley did not regularly break their messages until 1942. In the end, there were about 30 different army, air and naval Enigma nets in general use.

Early in the war, many naval messages still remained unreadable. Although some other simple naval codes could be read almost daily, Enigma encryptions could not yet be interpreted with any consistency. The non-Enigma messages did have their uses. For example, a certain German officer in the North African campaign reported daily with utmost regularity that he had nothing to report—a useless piece of information to his superiors, but of great value to the Bletchley operators. And then there was the Dockyard Cipher System, which at first seemed unsolvable, until a captured document provided the lead. The Dockyard Cipher served not only for messages to and from shipyards but also to and from many smaller vessels, such as patrol boats and auxiliaries. Moreover, the messages sent by the Dockyard system repeated virtually the same content both to vessels that had Enigma on board and also to those that did not. So there was another source of what was known as "cribs," shortcuts to reading the message, or "kisses," solving an easier system as a means of attempting to solve a more difficult one. It is thought that, following the sinking of the *Hood,* a successful decryption using Ultra contributed to locating the *Bismarck* on 27 May 1941. The ship was on its way to France and safety, when some messages regarding its location were decrypted and she was sunk.

The decryptions were translated into English and forwarded to the British armed services. For obvious reasons, particular interest was given to the information provided by Bletchley's naval section, such as weather reports, damage to German merchant shipping, dates of departures and returns of U-boats, and data on troop transports. They were sent by teleprinter to the Naval Intelligence Division (NID) in the Admiralty. NID, with fairly inadequate information at first, tried to track U-boats in the North Atlantic to prevent them from attacking convoys, Britain's lifelines. From January to March 1941, German submarines were sinking more ships than were being built in Britain and the United States. It was feared that if this continued, Britain would lose the battle of the Atlantic and probably the war. Reading and understanding Enigma messages was therefore essential.

At first, the Admiralty mistrusted the information from Ultra decrypts. An example of this, with disastrous consequences, was the case of the battleship *Tirpitz.* While *Tirpitz* was still lying in a Norwegian port, Ultra messages reported that the ship was not an immediate threat. But Admiral Sir Dudley Pound, the First Sea Lord and the head of the Royal Navy, did not trust this intelligence and scattered the precious convoy *PQ-17* fearing that the *Tirpitz* might attack. The result was that twenty-three out of thirty-four merchantmen were picked off by U-boats and the Luftwaffe, with a great loss of lives, military supplies, tanks, and other war material.

Apart from Enigma, there were other sources for gauging the enemy's intentions. German radio signals were monitored for Enigma intercepts. A sudden increase in radio traffic often provided a hint that something unusual was going on. A good example of this was the traffic analysis report by Harry Hinsley, a young codebreaker at Bletchley, prior to the German invasion of Norway, revealing that there was increased naval activity off Denmark and in the Baltic. Unfortunately, this information was ignored by the Office of Naval Intelligence, which did not recognize it as being a hard fact. When the Norwegian expedition failed, the Admiralty continued to ignore the traffic analysis report of increased German activity in the area. As a result, the British aircraft carrier *Glorious* and her two destroyer escorts were sunk by the *Scharnhorst* and the *Gneisenau* on 8 June 1940, with the loss of 1,519 men. Later, Hinsley, in chronicling the event in his book, *British Intelligence in the Second World War* (London, 1988), mentions the warning given to the Admiralty. However, the Ministry of Defence, in a further attempt at a cover-up, continued to claim, "British intelligence sources failed to discover that the German force had sailed." This is another example of the tendency at the Admiralty at the time to dismiss any information that had not originated with them.

The British commando raid on the Lofoten Islands in March 1941 yielded some keying documents and two Enigma rotor wheels taken from the abandoned trawler *Krebs*, but that was still insufficient. If there were decrypts of naval Enigmas, they were rare and sometimes came with a delay of two weeks—too late to be used effectively for British operations.

In May 1941, the capture of U-110 south of Greenland, with a fully operational Enigma machine on board together with charts, code books, and cipher keys for May and June, allowed Bletchley to penetrate the general-purpose cipher "Hydra" used by most German ships, including U-boats at that time. It also helped to decipher some Mediterranean Enigma nets and was used successfully until the end of the war. The deciphering of Hydra was a major victory in the battle of codebreaking.

DF (direction finding) was also helpful in tracking U-boats. A number of DF stations were placed along the British coast, from the Shetlands to Land's End, in Gibraltar, and later in Iceland. When a U-boat was sending a radio message, the DF station would take a bearing on it; if it lasted long enough, several other DF stations would also take bearings. The crossing point would be the location of the U-boat. Unfortunately, exact locations of the U-boats were not very accurate and, considering that the U-boat was in constant motion, any information as to its location very soon became obsolete. German weather reports were crucial for carrying out the war—first from aircraft, which were not sufficiently accurate, then from weather ships stationed in the North Atlantic, north of Iceland, and also from U-boats. The abbreviated weather messages were transmitted through Enigma. Because the weather ships were at sea for long periods of time, they usually used the same cipher net keys for two months. So Bletchley originated the idea of capturing a weather ship, which was approved by the OIC. In this way, the weather ships *München* and *Lauenberg* were captured with a good crop of keying documents. These were significant "pinches," but they provided only limited information. The struggle for Enigma decrypts in the battle of the Atlantic seemed to be on a seesaw. Throughout 1942 and early 1943, whenever Enigma could not be read consistently, the number of sinkings rose alarmingly.

As early as September 1940, when the British could read naval Enigma messages only intermittently and the situation seemed desperate, one especially cunning "pinch" had been planned by none other than Ian Fleming, future creator of James Bond. Fleming, who was in naval intelligence at that time, proposed a wild scheme. The purpose was to obtain an Enigma machine with codebooks from a German rescue boat in the English Channel. The plan was that British servicemen, pretending to be downed German pilots, would attract a German rescue boat, then overpower and kill the boat's crew. The scheme was accepted, code-named "Operation Ruthless," but later abandoned as impractical.

After the United States joined the war in December 1941, the waters off its East Coast became a happy hunting ground for German U-boats, as Americans did not introduce convoys for several months and ships were sunk by the dozen. But by the end of June 1941, the number of bombes manufactured by Bletchley rose to eight and, by mid-August, messages were solved every day, most of them within thirty-six hours. From the beginning, Churchill placed great importance on Enigma intercepts. Every day he had a selected number presented to him and was guided by the information provided in them. On his visit to Bletchley in September 1941, he praised Bletchley cryptanalysts and called them "the geese that laid the golden eggs and never cackled." From mid-1943, however, the Allies could systematically read the German navy's Enigma radio traffic, whereas the Germans were unable to break the new British Admiralty's codes and ciphers. This success in the struggle for secrets made it possible to locate precisely and sink numerous German U-boats as well as the tankers (the "milk cows") that supplied them at sea. When the U.S. entered the war in December 1941, subsequent British-American cooperation included naval Enigma intelligence, which was successfully used in many operations against Nazi submarines and other vessels, for example, in U.S. Navy and Air Force operations against the Kriegsmarine from June to October 1943 in the vicinity of the Azores. As a result of that action, conducted almost entirely on the basis of Enigma data, at least nineteen U-boats and all but one of the "milk cows" were sunk. The Nazi submarine command (*Befehlshaber der U-boote*) ordered detailed investigations, including the possibility that the enemy were decrypting German signals. Fortunately for the Allies, the Germans considered the possibility that the enemy had cracked the Enigma cipher to be improbable and once again discarded it.

The U-boat war in the Atlantic had its ups and downs. Admiral Doenitz's tactic of wolf packs had been very successful in 1942 and the beginning of 1943. In 1942, six million tons of shipping was sunk by U-boats. At the start of that year the total number of U-boats was 249, and at the end they numbered 393, so that in spite of some U-boat sinkings and the best efforts of the Allies, they were continually increasing in numbers. According to information provided by the submarine tracking room at the Admiralty, in the first three weeks of March 1943, 70 U-boats were operating in the Atlantic alone.

Although the German naval codes were much more difficult to decipher than those of the Luftwaffe and Wehrmacht, in December 1942, British cryptanalysts at Bletchley succeeded in breaking "Triton," the U-boat four-wheeled Enigma key. At first it was read intermittently but, by August 1943, the British were able to read Enigma traffic with little or no delay so that it could be used in operations. This information provided the Admiralty with vital intelligence regarding the departure times and dates of U-boats to and from their bases, the number and type of U-boats at sea, and the movements and dispositions of their patrol groups and their operational orders. Admiral Doenitz believed that his U-boat losses from air attacks (frequently at night) at that time were due to Allied aircraft homing in on the emitted radiation from U-boat radars. He could not conceive that the losses were mainly due to Enigma decrypts.

In order to conceal the fact that the British sometimes had very precise intelligence from Ultra, it was necessary not to make direct operational use of this information without an appropriate cover. For instance, when the location of a German convoy became known through Ultra, a spotter plane would be sent up to circle the convoy at a safe distance prior to the planned Allied attack, giving the impression that this was how the convoy was discovered.

With the new 10-cm radar, invisible to the Germans, reinforcement of escort carriers, the Very Long Range Aircraft, improvement in Coastal Command, and the tactics of warships protecting convoys, the British gained the upper hand. In the course of April and May 1943, Doenitz lost 56 U-boats. This made him withdraw his U-boat fleet westward of the Azores.

From intercepted Ultra signals it became evident that U-boat crews were losing morale. It was not surprising as, out of the total of 40,000 U-boat sailors, about three-quarters lost their lives during the war. During June, July, and August of 1943, in the Bay of Biscay and elsewhere more U-boats were sunk than Allied merchant vessels: 74 versus 58. So U-boats became an acceptable threat, unlike that posed by big ships such as *Bismarck, Scharnhorst,* and *Gneisenau* which, when let loose on the oceans, could play havoc with convoys of merchant shipping crisscrossing the Atlantic. The Allies simply could not pro-vide a sufficiently powerful escort to defend every convoy from this menace.

Even though the Germans believed that Enigma was unbreakable, they used, at the highest level only, another cipher machine called the "Geheimschreiber" ("secret writing machine"), which was considered by them to be even safer than Enigma. It resembled Enigma in principle but was much larger. It had ten rotors, all rotating simultaneously. It automatically enciphered a signal typed out in the clear and sent it to telegraph or radio stations at the rate of 62 words per minute, and it did not need a cipher clerk. In order to receive a message at the other end, a similar machine was needed, which automatically typed out the text. In effect, it was a teleprinter. In function, it resembled a typewriter more than an Enigma machine in that it contained 32 separate elements against Enigma's 26 letters. In addition, it had ten numbers, punctuation, a teleprinter function, and other features.

The British had no end of trouble with it. They worked on this machine at Bletchley from the beginning of the war but made little headway, until they seized two of them in North Africa and managed to build a similar one code-named "Fish." But it was still necessary to find out every day what the key setting was for the rotors, the combinations of which reached into billions. Then, by using Turing's ideas for the creation of an artificial brain, together with those of Prof. Max Newman, a mathematician from Cambridge, the "Oriental Goddess" was constructed. This machine was capable of scanning 2,000 telegraphic signals per second, using for the first time the electronic principles of breaking codes based on a statistical system. This device was not very successful, however, as it overheated and was too slow. An improved version called "Colossus Mark I" was built. It boasted 1,500 electronic valves and could read 5,000 symbols per second. Eventually, in 1944, "Mark II" was built. This one had 2,500 valves and could read 25,000 symbols per second. It was in place in time for the invasion of the European continent on 6 June 1944.

"OVERLORD" AND THE ALLIED OFFENSIVE IN FRANCE

In January 1943, General Frederick Morgan was assigned as Chief of Staff to the Supreme Allied Commander (COSSAC) to set up planning for "Overlord," the Allied invasion of France. Of special value for the planning work of COSSAC were numerous Enigma decrypts about changes in the strength and location of the Wehrmacht armored and motorized divisions in France, and about the construction of the German fortifications (the "Atlantic Wall"). Enigma was also essential for carrying out various camouflage and deception operations, aimed at supplying the German High Command with a misleading picture of the Allied military buildup in Britain for the coming invasion. Ultra remained a principal source of strategic intelligence after the Supreme Headquarters, Allied Expeditionary Forces (SHAEF), headed by General Eisenhower, had been created in February 1944.

The Allied invasion in Normandy on 6 June 1944 opened a new phase of the war. Soon the Enigma messages read at Bletchley confirmed the fact that the Allied deception operations had been effective and that the area of the landings was a complete surprise for the Germans. It was not until the evening of the sixth that Hitler released his armored divisions held in reserve to the high command in the West. After the Allied forces were securely ashore, the most spectacular effect of the Enigma intelligence was the air strike on the tenth, which paralyzed strong German armored forces, the Panzergruppe West, for a fortnight. Another major Enigma contribution was the warning of the imminent attack of the German Seventeenth SS Panzer Division at Carentan on 13 June; this signal proved vital in the capture of Cherbourg by the U.S. troops. Highly significant also were the decrypted messages stating that the II Panzer Corps had been moved from the Russian front to France to dislodge the invaders. As a result of this information, the Allies were able to prevent these new German forces from taking part in the battle to cross the Odon River, and also to halt a strong counterattack by the Nineteenth SS Panzer Division on 9 July. "In all three cases," writes Ralph Bennett in his monograph on the Normandy invasion, "Ultra prompted actions which had a most important bearing on the progress of the campaign."

Ultra information was also behind many decisions taken during two major Allied operations, namely, "Cobra," the American breakout at the end of July 1944, and the battle of the Falaise pocket, in which the Polish First Armored Division played an essential role. Bletchley's decrypting work contributed largely to the success of General Bradley's plan ordering General Patton's armor to advance up the Loire valley. As the scale of operations grew, so did the scale of the Enigma contribution. Exact radio intelligence and the reading of enemy signals were largely responsible in the next few weeks for the swift advance of the Allied armies across northern France.

However, when the Allied offensive came to a halt in September 1944, as Ralph Bennett (*Ultra in the West*) stated: "striking instances of the disregard of Ultra on matters of first-rate importance begin to accumulate." An explicit Enigma warning about the arrival in the region of Arnhem of two SS Panzer Divisions had been overlooked by Allied high commands, resulting in their combined land-air operation, "Market-Garden," ending in tragedy. In late September 1944 and during the next weeks, there were again many hints from radio intelligence of a forthcoming German counterattack in the Ardennes. The German forces were able to mount a surprise offensive in December 1944 and make initial progress only because of the state of euphoria, which existed among many Allied commanders, stemming from their conviction that the war was already won. But especially after the start of a new sweeping Russian offensive in January 1945, no local Nazi success could change any more the ultimate outcome of the war, and the German assault in the West came to a halt.

GERMAN V1 AND V2 WEAPONS

The first Enigma reports concerning the German V1 and V2 weapons appeared early in 1943 with a message ordering special anti-aircraft protection for the Peenemunde station, code-named "FZG76," on the Baltic Sea. After further intelligence data from Enigma, air reconnaissance, and other sources had been collected, Peenemunde was bombed on the night of 17/18 August 1943, and the heavy damage inflicted set back the production of the V1 flying bombs for six months.

Enigma decrypts on V weapons returned when the experimental launching site for V1 and V2 missiles was transferred to Blizna in south-central Poland. In April 1944, Enigma produced Hitler's order to establish a special headquarters near Amiens in France to manage the V1 operations. At the end of May 1944 an Enigma message reported that fifty sites were ready for launching. On D-Day, 6 June, the commander of the V1 units in France received orders for an immediate all-out offensive to start on the twelfth. At it happened, the first V1 landed on the thirteenth, and from then on all German signals about V1s and V2s were carefully followed up at Bletchley in order to make it easier for Allied air forces to combat them. Fighter pilots shot down V1s also in flight; Polish pilots alone destroyed some 190 flying bombs.

Despite the effectiveness of this new and terrifying attack, no *Wunderwaffe* ("miracle weapon") of Hitler's could withstand the Allied offensive and the joint force of the Great Anti-Nazi Coalition.

Conclusion

It was only after books on the subject of Enigma appeared in the 1970s and 1980s, as well as a few others that were published since, that reliable information about the history of Enigma and Ultra came to light. On the whole, books in the early 1970s contained many inaccuracies regarding the Polish contribution to the solution of the Enigma code. For example, Winterbotham and Stevenson give ill-informed accounts of how the Enigma machine was first obtained. And Stevenson, in his paperback edition of *A Man called Intrepid,* refers to Rejewski as "mademoiselle Marian Rejewski," indicating some measure of careless research. Those misleading accounts were later repeated by others and accepted as the truth. Even Welchman, who is the most accurate on the subject, admitted to a number of errors in his first edition of *The Hut Six Story* (1982). As he explained later, he lacked knowledge of the whole picture at the time. However, he corrected these errors—having to do mostly with his attribution of work on Enigma to the British rather than the Poles—in a paper published in 1986 and in the new edition of his book published in 1998. In the foreword of that later edition, Alan Stripp justifies these errors by the fact that, prior to the 1980s, few people knew of the achievements of the Polish cryptologists. Until that time, all participants were bound by the Official Secrets Act: the Public Record Office did not make any of the information available. It is therefore not surprising that what information there is, even now, is often intentionally or unconsciously distorted.

Books in the late 1970s and 1980s give a truer picture of the achievements of the Polish cryptologists, unlike the daily press that perpetuated early misinformation and tended to diminish the role of the Poles. According to S. Nowodworski, in his article in London's *Dziennik* of 14 December 2000, articles in the recent press frequently implied that the Poles owed their successes either: to the information provided to them by the French intelligence service; to errors committed by the German operators; or else, to pure, sheer luck. No mention was made at that time, however, of the fact that from the outset the French and British cipher services were in possession of the very same information, the only difference being that, unlike the Poles, they did not know how to use it to their advantage. Of course, this does not detract from the later British achievements in solving new complicated Enigma problems caused by the Germans' obsessively frequent changes and improvements made to the German machine, even though, as far as it is known, they did not suspect that their code had been broken.

John R. Colville in his book, *Strange Inheritance*, claims that the main source of weakness of the British intelligence services was the envy and rivalry among the different agencies in England—the naval, army and air intelligence services, the Secret Intelligence Service, etc.—as well as with Allied intelligence services. The Poles disclosed all they knew to their British ally in their joint war against Hitler, while the British saw in the Polish intelligence services a rival competing for credit in intelligence achievements. On the other hand, restriction of information to the highest ranks of British command on the "need to know" basis was essential for the effective and secure conduct of war operations. Obviously the greater was the number of individuals who knew of the existence of Ultra the greater was the danger of a leak.

The evidence of Polish input into wartime intelligence seems to have disappeared in the British records. All original records of Polish decrypts of Enigma as well as all archives of Polish intelligence that had been handed over to the British at the end of the war are either well hidden or destroyed. In July 1999, Ms. T. A. Sterling, chief of

Historical Bureau and Archives of the British Cabinet, in accounting for the disappearance of those records, stated that they were "ephemeral in nature" and were therefore not worth keeping (Nowak Jezioranski, *New Horizon*, 3 September 1999.)

Another instance of the British tendency to dismiss or neglect to mention in their records other than their own intelligence sources—in spite of their normally meticulous record of their own achievements—is evident in the five-volume *British Intelligence in the Second World War,* in which merely a passing reference is made to the fact that the first reports of rocket-testing in Peenemunde were supplied at great personal risk by the Poles.

Not only were errors made of omission but also of commission, as evidenced in the recent British film, *Enigma,* based on the 1995 thriller written by Robert Harris. In this film, supposedly historically correct and attempting to give an impression of a documentary, a Pole working at Bletchley Park is portrayed as a traitor to the British cause when he divulges to the Germans the breaking of the Enigma code by the British. According to A. Swidlicki (*Nowy Dziennik*, 2 October 2001), the Poles, none of whom ever worked at Bletchley Park, protested to Robert Harris and to the filmmakers, but to no avail. Harris claimed poetic license in the addition of fictional touches to make the book more appealing to readers. Prof. Norman Davies considers the film to be dishonest and harmful to the Poles. In his letter to the *Daily Telegraph* of 27 September 2001, he wrote that the filmmakers and the scriptwriter Tom Stoppard interpreted historical truths very freely. So did the Hollywood producers in the making of the fictional film, *U-571* (in which Americans capture an Enigma machine from a German submarine), at which the British were justly offended, this having been their exploit!

Some of the British authors are of the opinion that British and Polish achievements in breaking the Enigma code are fairly comparable, making light of the fact that the Poles owed their success solely to three men who established the theoretical basis for solutions and provided the required bombes, cyclometers, and perforated sheets with minimal financial and technical support, while the British effort which followed had infinitely greater backing of money, human resources, and technical know-how.

Other authors had a different view of the role of the Poles. Welchman, for example, claimed that the "numinous presence of the Polish cryptographers haunted all subsequent British achievements in this area," and that without the Polish initial solutions British success at Bletchley Park would be doubtful; thus the Battle of Britain and the Battle of the Atlantic would perhaps not have been won. This view is supported by Maurice Freedman in his book, *Unravelling Enigma* (Pen & Sword Books, 2000), in which he claims that without the success achieved by the Poles initially, Bletchley Park would not have been able to break the Enigma code at the start of 1940. And later on, the success achieved in reading Ultra messages made it possible to convince the mistrustful admirals, generals, and civil service chiefs that crucial information about enemy intentions provided in the deciphered Enigma messages needed to be centralized and distributed to all services instead of each service doing this work on its own and jealously guarding the results. Therefore, as Freedman suggests, not only were the Poles instrumental in influencing the outcome of the Battle of Britain and the Battle of the Atlantic but also in establishing a better system of distribution of intelligence.

David A. Hatch, an American cryptology expert at the Center of Cryptologic History, NSA Fort George G. Meade, Maryland, wrote (*Naród Polski,* 17 December 1998*),* "The breaking of the Enigma by Poland was one of the cornerstones of the Allied victory over Germany."

It can be said that with Ultra the battle of the Atlantic was won. Also, to a considerable degree it played a part in the success of the North African campaign and the Normandy invasion. There are, of course, many factors that contributed to the shortening of the war, but it is widely believed that Ultra saved the world at least two years of war and possibly prevented Hitler from winning. So far, only a small part of the Enigma documents has been made available for research. It is increasingly felt by historians that, while the history of the Second World War may not have to be completely rewritten, much of it will definitely need to be reexamined.

Epilogue

Something should be said about what happened after the war to the people who for many years, from 1929 through 1945, were involved in the great Allied Enigma operation.

Gustave Bertrand, who repeatedly influenced the fate of the Polish cryptologists, remained in military service after May 1945 and became a general in the French army. General Charles de Gaulle awarded him the highest French decoration, the "Grand Officier de la Légion d'Honneur." After his retirement from the army, he became mayor of the town of Théoule-sur-Mer in southern France, where he died in 1976.

The three young men who gave the British such a valuable gift in the solution of Enigma did not gather much recognition for their feat. Jerzy Różycki was lost at sea in January 1942 while returning from Algiers to France on SS *Lamoricière*, which sank when it hit a reef or mine. As noted, upon their arrival in Great Britain, in 1943 Rejewski and Zygalski were shunted away from Bletchley to do minor work on low-level codes. It was only toward the end of the war that the two, who were civilians until then, were made lieutenants in the Polish army.

Henryk Zygalski remained in England after the war, where he taught at the Battersea Technical College and also at the University of Surrey. He was awarded an honorary doctorate by a Polish scientific body in Britain. He died near Plymouth, England, in 1978.

Marian Rejewski, the most accomplished of the three, returned to Poland in November 1946. The rest of his career, in spite of his many talents, was unremarkable because of the political situation in postwar Poland: in communist Poland, it would have been unwise of him to dwell on his cryptological wartime achievements. When he received some recognition for his Enigma work, after 1973, with the publication of books by Bertrand and later Winterbotham, Rejewski gave numerous interviews to whoever expressed interest in his or his colleagues' achievements. However, he was a modest person who was not interested in the trappings of fame. His several distinctions (all Polish) were the Gold Cross of Merit, the Silver Cross of Merit with Swords, and the Army Medal. In addition, he received the prestigious Officers Cross of the Order of Polonia Restituta in August 1978, but refused the honorary doctorate and professorship proposed to him at that time. Of the three Polish mathematicians, he was the only one who received a measure of recognition in his lifetime, and that in Poland only. He died in Warsaw on 13 February 1980 and was buried with military honors at Warsaw's Powązki Cemetery.

In 1983, fifty years after Enigma was solved, a commemorative postage stamp was issued in Poland with pictures of the famous trio of codebreaking mathematicians on the special first-day cover (FDC) envelope.

Ronald Lewin dedicates his book, *Ultra Goes to War,* "To the Poles who sowed the seed and to those who reaped the harvest." These are the people whose story Lewin's book recounted.

Bibliography

Beesly, P. *Very Special Intelligence: The Story of the Admiralty's Operational Intelligence Centre 1939–45*. London: Hamish Hamilton, 1977.

Bennett, R. *Ultra in the West: The Normandy Campaign of 1944–45*. London: Hutchinson, 1979.

Bertrand, G. *Enigma, ou la plus grande énigme de la guerre 1939–1945*. Paris: Librairie Plon, 1973.

Budiansky, Stephen. *Battle of Wits*. New York: The Free Press, 2000.

Cairncross, John. *The Enigma Story*. London: Century, 1997.

Calvocoressi, P. *Top Secret Ultra*. New York: Pantheon Books, 1980.

Erskine, R. & Smith, M., eds. *Action This Day*, London: Bantam Press, 2001.

Freedman, Maurice. *Unravelling Enigma*. Barnsley, England: Pen & Sword Books, Leo Cooper, 2000.

Gaj, K. *Szyfr Enigmy—Metody Złamania*. Warsaw: Wyd. Komunikacji i Łączności, 1989.

Garliński, J. *Intercept: the Enigma War*. London: J. M. Dent and Sons Ltd, 1979.

Hinsley, F. H., et al. *British Intelligence in the Second World War*. London: Her Majesty's Stationery Office (vol. 1, 1979; vol. 2, 1981; vol. 3/1 1984; vol. 3/2 1988; vol. 4 1990; vol. 5, 1990).

Jones, R. V. *Most Secret War.* London: Hamish Hamilton, 1978.

Kahn, D. *The Codebreakers.* New York: Macmillan, 1967.

———. *Seizing the Enigma.* Boston: Houghton Mifflin, 1991.

Kapera, L. J. *Before ULTRA There was GALE.* Cracow: The Enigma Press, 2002.

Kippenhahn, Rudolf. *Code-breaking.* English translation. New York: The Overlook Press, 1999.

Kozaczuk, W. *Bitwa o tajemnice: Służba wywiadowcza Polski i Rzeszy Niemieckiej 1922–1939.* Warsaw: Książka i Wiedza, 1967, 4th ed. 1977.

———. *Enigma: How the German Machine Cipher was Broken, and How It Was Read by the Allies in World War II.* Edited and translated by C. Kasparek. Frederick, MD: University Publications of America, Inc., 1983.

———. *W Kręgu Enigmy.* Warsaw: Książka i Wiedza, 1979.

Kuratowski, K. *A Half Century of Polish Mathematics.* Oxford: Pergamon Press, 1980.

Lewin, R. *Ultra Goes to War.* London: Hutchinson, 1978.

Lisicki, Tadeusz. *Kombatant w Ameryce,* article in May/August 2000 issue (in Polish).

Paillole, P. *Services spéciaux 1935–45.* Paris: Robert Laffont, 1975.

Rejewski, M. *An Application of the Theory of Permutations in Breaking the Enigma Cipher.* Applicationes Mathematicae, XVI, no. 4. Warsaw, 1980.

———. *How Polish Mathematicians Deciphered the Enigma,* Annals of the History of Computing, vol. 3, no. 3, July 1981.

Rohwer, J., and Jackel, E., eds. *Die Funkaufklarung und ihre Rolle im Zweiten Weltkrieg.* Stuttgart: Motorbuch Verlag, 1979.

Rygor-Słowikowski, M. Z. *W tajnej służbie.* London: Mizyg Press, 1979; English version adapted by J. Herman. *In the Secret Service, The Lighting of the Torch.* London: The Windrush Press, 1988.

Santoni, A. *Il vero traditore: Il ruolo documentato di Ultra nella guerra del Mediterraneo.* Milan: Ugo Mursia, 1981.

Sebag-Montefiore, H. *Enigma.* New York: John Wiley & Sons, 2000.

Stevenson, W. *A Man Called Intrepid: The Secret War.* New York: Ballantine Books, 1978.

Welchman, G. *The Hut Six Story: Breaking the Enigma Codes.* New York: McGraw-Hill, 1982. 2nd ed. Cleobury Mortimer, England: M & M Baldwin, 1998.

Winterbotham, F. W. *The Ultra Secret.* London: Weidenfeld and Nicolson, 1974.

Woytak, R. A. *On the Border of War and Peace: Polish Intelligence and Diplomacy and The Origins of the Ultra Secret.* New York: Columbia University Press, 1979.

German high school diploma of Marian Rejewski in Bydgoszcz, 1917. (Ranked fourth out of forty-eight students.)

Marian Rejewski's M.Phil. Diploma (Mathematics) from the University of Poznań, 1 March 1928.

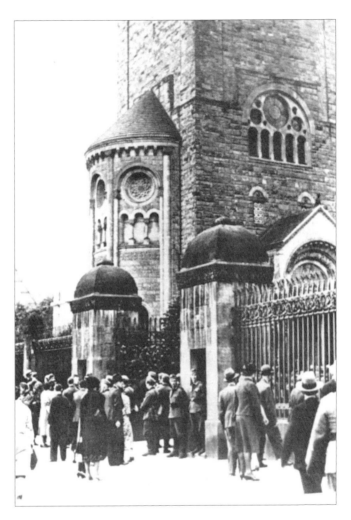

University of Poznań.

Polish General Staff Building (the Saxon Palace) in Warsaw in 1939.

Prewar Photos of the Polish Enigma Team

Maj. Maksymilian Ciężki.

Marian Rejewski.

Jerzy Różycki.

Henryk Zygalski.

Ludomir Danilewicz.

Leonard Danilewicz.

Antoni Palluth.

Edward Fokczyński.

Czesław Betlewski.

Maksymilian Ciężki before the war.

Major Ciężki in Britain after the war.

Maksymilian Ciężki with parents and sister on vacation.

Signature du Titulaire :
Podpis właściciela.

Maksymilian Ciężki in France (1940–42).

LEFT:
Maj. Gwido Langer before 1930.

BELOW:
Major Langer, in Britain, 1945, after return from German POW Camp.

Major Langer in "Cadix" (1940–42).

Henryk Zygalski and sister Monica (1918–19).

Henryk Zygalski before the war.

Henryk Zygalski in Cambridge, England.

Henryk Zygalski in England, after the war. He died in 1978.

Henryk Zygalski and wife, England, 1960s.

Merit certificate for Henryk Zygalski from Polish University in Exile, 1977.

Marian Rejewski's mother, Matilda.

Marian Rejewski's wife, Irena.

*Marian Rejewski with
son Andrzej, who died
in 1947.*

Irena Rejewska with children, in 1944.

Marian Rejewski's identity card as senior accountant, 1955, Bydgoszcz.

Marian Rejewski and grandson Wojtek.

*Irena and
Marian Rejewski
with Wojtek.*

*Marian Rejewski,
Warsaw, shortly before
his death in 1980.*

Memorial plaque in Bydgoszcz.

(a)

(b)

Polish reconstruction of the German machine, keyboard in alphabetical order; open (a) and closed (b).

*Replica of Enigma made by
Poles in France.
(1) Letter keys.
(2) Bulbs.
(3) Spare parts.
(4) Entry rotor.
(5) Three operational rotors
with rings.
(6) Reflector.
(7) Plugs.*

Secret Wehrmacht documents on Enigma (1935–36).

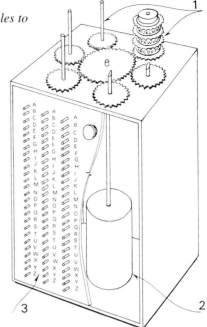

*A so-called "bombe" made by the Poles to speed up deciphering the Enigma.
(1) Enigma rotor; only one shown.
(2) Electric motor.
(3) Three rows of switches.*

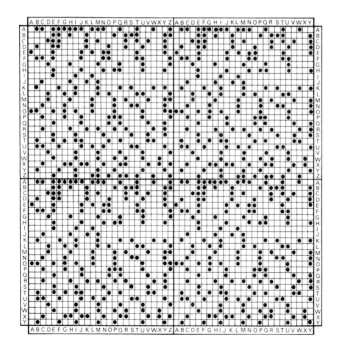

A perforated sheet to facilitate decoding.

Capt. Henri Braquenie (first left), French cryptologist at "Bruno" center in Gretz-Armainvillers, outside of Paris.

Gen. Stewart Menzies, head of British Secret Service.

Gen. Louis Rivet, head of French Secret Service.

Letter, dated 1 August 1939, to Polish mathematicians from Alfred D. Knox, Britain's senior cryptologist, thanking them for their cooperation and patience (in Polish).

Lt. Col. Gwido Langer, commander of the Polish section; Lt. Col. Gustave Bertrand, commander of "Bruno"; and visiting British representative Kenneth Macfarlane.

One of the buildings at "Bruno" center (Chateâu de Vignolles).

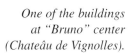

German Enigma in action (1942).

*German Enigma
in the field.*

Gen. Heinz Guderian in his command vehicle.

Sample text for training radio operators and cryptologists on Enigma.

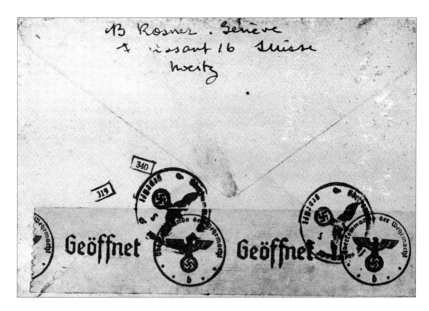

Rejewski's letter to his family in Poland (with a fictitious return address) censored by the Germans.

6. Signale für Wettermeldungen.

Standort und Flughöhe bei jeder Wettermeldung angeben.

Bei Flug unterhalb von Wolken.

Gute Sicht

		Astra
y a c	oberhalb Flugzeug wolkenlos oder einzelne Wolken	1
y a i	oberhalb Flugzeug stark bewölkt	2
y a m	oberhalb Flugzeug geschlossene Wolkendecke	3

Geringe Erdsicht infolge Dunstes oder Bodennebelnester

y a t	oberhalb Flugzeug wolkenlos oder einzelne Wolken	4
y a u	oberhalb Flugzeug stark bewölkt	5
y a x	oberhalb Flugzeug geschlossene Wolkendecke	6

10

Geringe Erdsicht infolge Niederschlag

y a y	einzelne Regen= oder Schneeschauer aus aufgerissener Wolkendecke	
y a z	gleichmäßiger Regen= oder Schneefall aus geschlossener Wolkendecke	
y b a	Eisregen	
y b b	starker Regen oder Hagelschauer infolge lokalen Gewitters	

Bei Flug oberhalb von Wolken oder zwischen zwei Wolkenschichten.

Erdsicht durch Lücken einer aufgebrochenen Wolkendecke

y b h	oberhalb Flugzeug wolkenlos oder einzelne Wolken	11
y b L	oberhalb Flugzeug stark bewölkt	12
y b m	oberhalb Flugzeug geschlossene Wolkendecke	13

Keine Erdsicht infolge geschlossenen Bodennebel=

y b n	oberhalb Flugzeug wolkenlos oder einzelne Wolken	14
y b o	oberhalb Flugzeug stark bewölkt	15
y b s	oberhalb Flugzeug geschlossene Wolkendecke	16

Luftwaffe's meteorological reports, which helped the Poles to break the Enigma.

Main building of the "Cadix" center in Uzès, (Chateâu de Fouzes) in southern France.

Polish cryptologists at "Cadix" From left: Marian Rejewski (first), Edward Fokczyński (second), Henryk Zygalski (fourth), Jerzy Różycki (sixth), Antoni Palluth (eighth).

From left: Piotr Smoleński, Jerzy Różycki, and Jan Graliński, who all perished in the sinking of SS Lamoricière in January 1942.

Gen. Gustave Bertrand after the war. He sent the photograph to Marian Rejewski with a dedication: "To my dear friend Marian Rejewski, one of the three discoverers of Enigma, as a memento of times past and with my best regards."

Spanish identity card, dated 14 June 1943, for Marian Rejewski then en route to England.

Headquarters building at Bletchley (Polish Festival in 2001).

In 1983 Poland commemorated the fiftieth anniversary of the breaking of the Enigma code by Polish mathematicians. Commemorative postage stamps.

Prince Andrew presents a copy of the Enigma machine to Polish Prime Minister Buzek as a symbol of importance of the role played by Poles in the war.

Used by permission of *Warsaw Voice*.

Appendix A

People of the Enigma: Jerzy Witold Różycki (1909–42)

by Zdzisław Jan Kapera
Translated by Tomasz Laczewski

Mathematician and cryptanalyst Jerzy Witold Różycki, also known by the pseudonym Julien Rouget, was born on 24 July 1909 in Olszana (a district of Kiev). He was the fourth and youngest child of Zygmunt, an apothecary (graduate of Petersburg University), and Wanda (née Benita). He died in 1942.

At first he attended the Polish "Borderland" ("Liceum Kresowe") secondary school in Kiev, but in 1918 he moved to Poland together with his parents. In 1926, Różycki finished secondary school in Wyszków on the Bug. He studied mathematics from 1927 until 1932 at the Institute of Mathematics of the Department of Science at Poznań University, and took his master's degree in mathematics under the direction of the outstanding scientist Zdzisław Krygowski on 19 February 1932. Owing to his extraordinary talents in mathematics and linguistics (and especially his proficiency in German), he was nominated by his professor to take part in a course of scientific foundations of cryptology, which was organized in 1929 by the General Staff's Cipher Bureau. From among more than twenty carefully chosen candidates, only three completed the course: Marian Rejewski, Henryk Zygalski, and Jerzy Różycki. Solution of a genuine Reichswehr message written in the most difficult code known during the First World War, the so-called "Doppelwürfelverfahren" (code of a double substitution, literally a Double Dice Cipher), settled his fate. In 1929, still as a student, he was employed by the

81

Poznań agency of the Cipher Bureau and on 1 September 1932, he was moved to Warsaw, to the BS4 Section (Biuro Szyfrów, German Cipher Office). His superiors were Capt. Maksymilian Ciężki and Maj. Gwido Langer. Różycki and his colleagues spent 1929 until the middle of 1932 examining the methods of encipherment used by the Reichswehr. He spent the second half of 1932 breaking the four-letter code of the German navy. It is worth mentioning that, while all the British achievements in this area during the First World War were based on captured German materials, Różycki and his colleagues succeeded in making correct guesses based upon their linguistic analyses. This allowed them gradually to reconstruct the entire code used by the Kriegsmarine in 1932. Most likely at the very beginning of 1933, Różycki was acquainted, by Marian Rejewski, with the theoretical base of the possibility of breaking the ciphers of the German ciphering machine Enigma. Using a ciphering machine adapted from the commercial type and its original day's keys unexpectedly supplied to the Poles by French intelligence (Gustave Bertrand), Różycki, together with Henryk Zygalski, were able for the first time to read German messages dating from September to October 1932, which had been intercepted by the Polish radio-intelligence. In this way, the theoretical reconstruction of the internal connections of Enigma that had been made by Rejewski were verified. Enigma stopped being a mystery, in spite of an astronomical number of possible combinations. However, constant changes perfecting the German machine forced Różycki and his colleagues to continue systematic work, which consisted of tracing and reconstructing the changes on the basis of mathematical calculations. In view of the complete (and intentional) destruction of Polish documents during evacuation in 1939, it is difficult nowadays to evaluate Różycki's precise personal contribution to the regular, daily identification of Enigma keys. But it is worth recalling that it was he who created a method, the so-called "clock method," which made it possible in many cases to determine which of the three cipher cylinders (wheels) was in position N, on the right side of the machine, on a given day. At first, the Germans changed the sequence of cylinders once a quarter, but from 1 January 1936, the change was made every month. His understanding of the system in itself shows how helpful Różycki's contribution to breaking Enigma was. We must mention that his linguistic talents helped him greatly in elaborating upon this method, which was extremely useful in the years 1933–38, when the efficiency of the BS4 group permitted systematic monitoring of German armaments and identification of newly formed units of the Wehrmacht and the Luftwaffe. Their codebreaking thus became a very important source of information for the General Staff and, by extension, for the Ministry of Foreign Affairs.

The secret work upon Enigma and the departure from Poznań in 1932 did not break Różycki's connections with his university. On 13 December 1937, he took another master's degree there, this time in geography.

In the face of impending war, on 25 and 26 July 1939, at Pyry near Warsaw, Różycki and his colleagues (with the assent of the Chief of the General Staff, Gen. Wacław Stachiewicz) acquainted French and English cryptanalysts with all their theoretical and mathematical achievements concerning Enigma. In retrospect, we must assess this step as very farsighted and effective: at that time, the French and English specialists were helpless against Enigma and were practically beginning their work from scratch. The outbreak of war stopped the work of BS4, and Różycki shared the fate of Langer's team. At first, during the evacuation of Poland, he was accompanied by his wife and son. But they parted—as it turned out forever—in Brześć. Różycki and his friends went through Łuck, Dubno, Krzemieniec, and Kuty to Bucharest, then to Paris. At the request of the French Service de Renseignements (with the assent of the Polish military authorities), he joined "Group Z" in the Section d'Examen of the Fifth Department of the French General Staff at Gretz-Armainvillers near Paris, which was dealing with breaking the radio communication of the German army and air force. Różycki's contribution to the work on Enigma in 1940 must have been considerable. As a member of a three-person team, he (together with his colleagues) read 1,152 encrypted messages during the Norwegian campaign and 5,048 during the French campaign. We can say with absolute conviction that, during the second half of the French campaign of 1940, the team he belonged to delivered to the command of the Allied armies current data about the German army and air force. No wonder the French evacuated the team to Oran, then to Algiers. After the creation of a "Free Zone" subordinated to the Vichy government, the French Resistance located the Polish team in Les Fouzes castle near Uzès, in Gard *département* (Provence). They formed the so-called "Field Station Office 300." Here, it seems, Różycki was still engaged upon Enigma's ciphers, but his cryptological interest broadened. With Zygalski and Rejewski, he broke a cipher used by the German occupying force for telegraphic communication. This was of crucial significance for the French Resistance and for the safety of the team of cryptanalysts as well. A great number of the messages (about six thousand) concerned the activities of the German police all over Europe: they revealed, among other things, the mass slaughter of the Jews in the eastern parts of Poland after 22 June 1941.

In the summer of 1941, Różycki was sent to Africa to decipher for the French the materials coming from the local French interception in Algiers. The idea was, first of all, to read the messages sent by the mixed German-Italian post of the Armistice Commission. He perished on his way back to France in the shipwreck of the SS *Lamoricière* near the Balearies.

Różycki's participation in elucidating the secrets of the Enigma was not revealed until 1973, when Gustave Bertrand's book was published. It was also confirmed by Rejewski's unpublished memoirs of September 1939 and the so-called Col. Stefan Mayer's memorandum. Nowadays Różycki is included among the world's outstanding cryptanalysts in the twentieth century. He is commemorated in a plate embedded in the building of the Institute of Mathematics at Poznań University. Różycki is also recalled in a story written by Strumph Wojtkiewcz, entitled *Enigma's Secret* (*Sekret Enigmy,* Warsaw 1978, 2nd ed. 1979), and in a film and a serial of the same title made under the direction of Roman Wionczek in 1979.

Różycki had married Maria Barbara Mayka in 1938. Their son Jan Janusz, born on 10 May 1939, graduated from the Academy of Fine Arts. A sportsman, Jan was a member of the Polish fencing team that won a silver medal at the Tokyo Olympics in 1964.

Bibliography

Manuscripts and Documents

Bertrand, G. *Declaration (á l'intention du B.H.A. polonais)* 5 October 1973.

Langer, G. *Sprawozdanie z pracy ekipy ppłk. dypl. Langera w czasie kampanii francuskiej, tj. 1 X 1939 do 24 VI 1940* and *Sprawozdanie dotyczące ewakuacji Ekspozytury Nr. 300,* London 10 July 1945 (cf. Polish Institute and Sikorski Museum A 12 24/68).

Mayer, S. A. *The breaking up of the German ciphering machine "Enigma" by the cryptological section in the 2nd Department of the Polish Armed Forces' General Staff,* London 31 May 1974 and *Supplement* 4 December 1974.

Rejewski, M. *Wspomnienia z mej pracy w Biurze Szyfrów Oddziału II Sztabu Głównego w latach 1930–1945,* Bydgoszcz, 1967 (cf. Wojskowy Instytut Historyczyny nr I/2/44).

Różycka, M. B. *Mgr Jerzy Witold Różycki,* Warszawa 20 July 1978 and *Wspomnienia żony kryptologa . . . z 1939 r.*

Books and Articles

Bertrand, G. *Enigma, ou la plus grande énigme de la guerre 1939–1945.* Paris: Plon, 1973.

Bloch, G. *"Enigma" avant "Ultra,"* Paris 1988 (revised edition, privately printed).

Gaj, K. *Szyfr Enigmy—Metody złamania.* Warszawa: Wydawnictwa Komunikacj i Łączności, 1989, cf. esp. pp. 120–23.

Garliński, J. *Intercept: Secrets of the Enigma War.* London: Dent, 1979.

Kapera, Z. J. *Raport polpułkownika Karola Gwidona Langera: Sojuszniczy radiowywiad w kampanii francuskiej 1940 r.,* "Studia Historyczne" (Cracow) 33, 1990, no. 1, pp. 115–34.

Kozaczuk, W. *Enigma: How the German Machine Cipher Was Broken and How It Was Read by the Allies in World War Two.* Frederick, MD: University Publications of America, 1985.

———. *W Kręgu Enigmy.* Warszawa: Książka i Wiedza, 1986.

Lisicki, T. *Die Leistung des polnischen Enzifferungsdienstes bei der Lösung des Verfahrens der deutschen "Enigma"-Funkschlüsselmaschine* [in:] *Die Funkaufklärung und Ihre Rolle im Zweiten Weltkrieg,* ed. by J. Rohwer, E. Jackel, Stuttgart: Motorbuch Verlag, 1979, pp. 66–86.

———. *Pogromcy Enigmy we Francji.* "Orzeł Biały." London, September 1975, pp. 8–10.

Paillole, P. *Notre espion chez Hitler.* Paris: Plon, 1985 [a part of the Mayer Memorandum concerning the French phase of the "Enigma" case is reprinted on pp. 266–68].

Rejewski, M. *Jak matematycy polscy rozszyfrowali Enigmę.* "Wiadomości Matematyczne." Warszawa 33, 1980, no. 1, pp. 1–28 [cf. pp. 3, 15, 19].

Rygor-Słowikowski, M. Z. *W tajnej służbie (In Secret Service),* London: Mizyg Press, 1977.

Woytak, R. A. *A Conversation with Marian Rejewski.* "Cryptologia" 6, 1982, pp. 50–60.

Appendix B

Before Enigma: Jan Kowalewski and the Early Days of the Polish Cipher Bureau (1919–22)

by Robert J. Hanyok

Modern cryptology in the early twentieth century was dominated by the exploits of a handful of pioneering individuals. These men and women—who were part savant, part autodidact, with some bits of visionary and buccaneer mixed in—came to define cryptology and the directions it took in the respective countries in which they worked. In the English-speaking countries of the United States and the British Commonwealth, we are mainly aware of such names as Yardley, the Friedmans (William and Elizabeth), Denniston, Tiltman, "Blinker" Hall, Agnes Driscoll, and Laurence Safford, among others. Sadly, outside of this narrow Anglo-American coterie, little is known of the work of early cryptologists from other countries. This is all the more our loss, because some of their stories are as interesting as those emanating from the United States and Great Britain. In many cases, these other individuals were well known to their Anglo-American counterparts, as allies or as adversaries. At the same time, these pioneers affected the history of their own countries as much as those in the United States and England. Of these cryptologists, one of the most fascinating is the Polish army officer, Jan (or Ian) Kowalewski, the founder of the Polish Cipher Bureau.

In trying to reconstruct Kowalewski's life, one of the major problems that one encounters is the lack of primary archival sources. The Nazi conquest of Poland is the main reason: the records of the Polish Cipher Bureau (Biuro Szyfrów) that the Germans did not capture were probably destroyed deliberately by the retreating Poles. Most of the Bureau's personnel (though not all) escaped to France, via Rumania, and later to England. After the war, Kowalewski stayed in Great Britain and edited a magazine on Central European affairs. What we know of his exploits comes from interviews with him and others from the Bureau. However, the anti-Soviet British writers who recorded his cryptologic achievements probably minimized the contributions of other Poles, as well as downplayed the influence of French and Japanese technical exchanges and training during the first days of the Cipher Bureau.[1] What has been recovered of his career and exploits is thus fragmentary and occasionally contradictory; no photograph of Kowalewski is readily available. Still, we can draw a good picture of one of this century's cryptologic pioneers.

Jan Kowalewski was born in 1892 in the city of Łódź, which is about sixty miles southwest of Warsaw, in the portion of eastern Poland that was part of the Czarist empire. Intelligent and talented, he, like many Poles at the turn of the century, was passionate about a free Poland. In 1911, Kowalewski went to Belgium to study chemical engineering. When the First World War broke out, he returned to Russia and took a commission in the Czar's army. At the time of the Bolshevik revolution in 1917, he was elected by a soldier's committee to command a unit. When Polish national units started to defect to the newly established state of Poland, Kowalewski marched west with them. There, he became a staff officer for General Józef Piłsudski, Poland's first head of state and a marshal of its armies.

In mid-1919, hoping to expand its territory (and recover portions of a "historic," greater Poland) at the expense of a Bolshevik Russia itself threatened by allied interventionist forces and the loose coalition of Russian counter-revolutionary forces, Poland invaded western Russia, seizing parts of Lithuania and Byelorussia.[2] At the time, the fledgling Bolshevik regime in Moscow could do nothing to stop the Poles since it was besieged from several points, the most dangerous being the Western powers–backed armies of the counter-revolutionaries, or "White" Russians, led by Generals Wrangel and Denikin and Admiral Kolchak. It was at this point that the most trivial of events happened that led to the start of the amazing cryptologic career of then-Lieutenant Kowalewski and the subsequent founding of the Polish Cipher Bureau.

As Kowalewski told it, one day a friend of his was getting married and asked him to fill in for a fortnight at his post in a radio station. At the site, Kowalewski's job was to review the station's intercept of foreign radio broadcasts and telegrams and to evaluate them, looking for anything of value to intelligence or propaganda. A master of several languages, Kowalewski easily took to the work and became intrigued by the job. One day, a radio operator handed him some coded Bolshevik messages that he had intercepted. Within two days, he broke the Bolshevik key—their systems were quite elementary, including simple codes and substitution/transposition ciphers, such as the "Caesar" system. What these messages revealed was the Bolsheviks' appreciation of the Whites' military situation. In this case, General Denikin's drive towards Moscow was being threatened (unknown to him) by two Bolshevik divisions that had been trailing him and were slipping behind his forces to cut their lines of communication.[3]

Kowalewski passed the information up the Polish chain of command to the intelligence branch of the General Staff in Warsaw. Excited that they could now keep an eye on both the Reds and Whites (at the time, the Poles actually feared the ultimate designs of the Whites more than they did those of the Reds, seeing that the Whites might try to reclaim portions of Poland for a reconstituted imperial Russia), Chief of Staff, General Rozwadowski, ordered Kowalewski to form an intercept-and-deciphering unit. The Polish Radio Telegraphic Department's entire broadcast monitoring staff was given to him while officers with foreign language and mathematics abilities were assigned to his new department.[4] To handle the enormous amounts of coded and enciphered Bolshevik military messages now being collected by the Polish radio intercept sites, a number of mathematicians were transferred to Kowalewski's burgeoning Cipher Bureau.[5]

By early 1920, the Poles could read nearly all of the Red Army's secret communications. The Poles were also helped by the policy of the Bolshevik Minister of Defense and Commissar of the Red Army, Leon Trotsky, who had ensured that his formations were well supplied with radios which, in turn, assisted Warsaw's intercept of Bolshevik messages.[6] However, Red Army communications and cipher security had not advanced much since the Czarist Imperial Army's disaster at Tannenberg in 1914. In that battle, Germany had exploited Russian communications to defeat its two armies in detail. Bolshevik ciphers remained simple substitution and transposition systems that were easily broken. The Polish Cipher Bureau had reached the point that intercepted messages were broken, translated, and reported to the Polish General Staff in the same day. The Polish military command had in its hands the strengths, plans, and shortcomings of Trotsky's military forces.

In March 1920, the Polish forces began the invasion of the Ukraine, hoping to detach this historically contested territory from Moscow. Marshal Piłsudski dreamed of forging an alliance of independent national states, such as Lithuania and the Ukraine, to oppose communist Russia, but this ambitious plan never had a chance to succeed. Even though his forces had reached the Ukrainian capital, Kiev, by May they were dangerously overextended. Having ignored warnings from Kowalewski's cryptologists of an impending Bolshevik riposte from the South, Piłsudski's troops found their lines of communications threatened and were forced into a hasty retreat back to Warsaw.[7] By summer, Trotsky had organized a massive counterattack by the Red Army. In the north, directly in line with Warsaw, was the Soviet Western Front with four armies under the command of General Mikhail Tukachevsky, perhaps Trotsky's most capable military leader. To the south, heading for Lublin, was General Semyon Budenny's Southwestern Front, composed of his battle-hardened cavalry troops with Joseph Stalin as its political commissar. To liaise between the two fronts, an ad hoc unit, the Mozyr Group (Mozyrskoya Gruppa), was organized. As long as the Mozyr Group held a front of thirty miles, there was no problem, for it could protect the vulnerable gap between the main two Red Army fronts. Moving inexorably westward, those two fronts pushed the defending Poles closer to the gates of Warsaw on the banks of the Vistula River. Behind the troops came a provisional Polish government under the charge of Feliks Dzherzinsky, a Polish communist and the head of Lenin's notorious secret police apparatus known as the Cheka. The Bolshevik leaders, flush with an impending victory and not unlike the Poles a few months earlier, had a greater ambition before their eyes—to carry the Bolshevik revolution into a fragile Germany and the rest of the weary, post-WWI Western Europe. But, as the Soviets closed on Warsaw and central Poland, their main forces drifted apart on separate axes of advance and the gap that the Mozyr Group had to cover dangerously widened.

As the Russian armies advanced westward, Kowalewski's radio men intercepted messages that revealed the Reds' order of battle, the locations of their various divisions, their avenues of attack, and even the new cryptographic keys for the Bolshevik ciphers. The most important information came from the Mozyr Group's commander who radioed that the gap between Tukachevsky's and Budenny's forces was too wide for him to cover with his meager force of cavalry troops.[8] The Cipher Bureau passed this information to the intelligence staff of Polish General Headquarters in Warsaw. When Piłsudski was told of the gap, he saw an opportunity to unhinge the Soviet advance by attacking through it and then swinging north behind Tukachevsky's lines of communication. He needed to know one more thing: were there any reserves to meet the proposed Polish counterattack? Kowalewski's answer was no.[9] Ignoring the advice of his French advisors, on 6 August 1920, Piłsudski ordered Polish units into the gap. The Mozyr Group was overwhelmed. Tukachevsky did not react for two days to the growing Polish threat to his rear because Kowalewski, in addition to his intercept work, had organized a massive jamming of all Fourth Army's radio communications utilizing the national network of Polish radio stations similar to the one that Kowalewski had started in the year before.[10] Totally confused and isolated, Tukachevsky's forces collapsed. Three of his armies disintegrated, and the fourth fled to Lithuania to be interned there.

To the south, a final, desperate riposte by Budenny's cavalry force to cut off the Polish breakthrough was stopped at Zamość. His mounted troops, who had harried Polish forces westward across the Ukraine all summer, were decisively stopped. This attack had been anticipated by Piłsudski, again; he had been tipped off by the reports of troop concentration by Kowalewski's bureau.[11]

In Polish history, this event became known as the "Miracle on the Vistula." Jan Kowalewski was awarded Poland's highest medal, the "Virtuti Militari," by Piłsudski himself. Yet, this was not the end of Kowalewski's cryptologic career. After the Russo-Polish war, Kowalewski's bureau found itself involved with major new targets such as Russian diplomatic maneuvers in the Baltic region and the secret rearming and training by the German Reichswehr. Poland's position between these two powers—each of which nursed a national grudge against Poland—mandated the expansion of the Cipher Bureau. To improve its capabilities, the Polish Cipher initiated a series of contacts with the cryptologic organizations of major powers. One natural choice was France with its history of tactical COMINT successes during the First World War. It is possible that French and Polish contacts had begun as early as 1919, during the war with Bolshevik Russia; there had been a large French military advisory mission in Warsaw during the conflict. In late 1920, senior Polish cryptologists began to go to Paris for formal training.

In 1922, the Poles approached the Japanese about technical exchanges. This feeler possibly was not the first meeting between the two countries on cryptologic issues. In 1920, even as the Bolshevik armies neared Warsaw, there is a suggestion that the Japanese had offered some technical advice or information on Soviet codes based on their own experience in the Far East[12]; then, again, the Poles, thanks to Kowalewski's bureau, already knew of the shortcomings in the Russian codes. However, in 1922, the Poles developed their own enticement for the Japanese: decrypts of Russian diplomatic messages relating to Soviet-Japanese negotiations over the port of Darien (known today as Dalien). Intrigued by the Polish successes against the Russians, the Japanese requested lectures and technical advice on cryptology. Kowalewski, who had just returned from Paris where he had taken a staff course on radio intelligence from the French military, was dispatched to Tokyo.

In Japan, Kowalewski, now a Captain, delivered a series of lectures to Japanese naval and army officers. Sitting in his audience among these officers were Commander Risaburo Ito, the future designer of the "Red" and "Purple" diplomatic machines, and Lieutenant Commander Nakasugi, who later organized the Imperial Japanese navy's first radio intelligence unit.[13] The main emphasis of Kowalewski's lectures was the development of codes and ciphers—cryptography—and the improvement of Japanese systems. He taught the Japanese how to strengthen ciphers by varying inscription and transcription methods, thus making stereotypical Japanese formats and text less susceptible to cribs. He also conducted cryptanalytic workshops for neophyte Japanese codebreakers using the United States State Department GRAY code for their exercises.[14]

Did his lectures help? Kowalewski told the story that, during a break in one of his lectures one day, he spotted Japanese officials burning up old papers and books in a courtyard of the building where he was teaching. He asked his interpreter what was happening. The response was that ever since his talks, the Japanese realized how poor their old codes and ciphers were, so they had begun destroying them and designing new ones.[15] Eventually, Kowalewski would receive a special bejeweled sword from the Japanese for his work.

Praise came from another, and unexpected quarter, as well. Herbert O. Yardley, the founder and head of the American "Black Chamber," a cryptologic office jointly funded by the U.S. State and War Departments, when working on Japanese army cipher systems at the time, had found a sudden increase in sophistication which required many months of work with "all our skill" to break. He attributed this increase to Kowalewski's work, though Yardley never mentioned his name and always referred to him as the "Polish cryptographer."[16]

However, upon returning from Japan with all these accomplishments, Captain Kowalewski, like some cryptologic Cincinnatus, just walked away from the Cipher Bureau. He took a staff position in Warsaw and then went on to be the Polish military attaché to Moscow and then Bucharest. He was never directly involved with cryptology again. Still, his legacy is impressive. He founded the Polish Cipher Bureau and gave it its initial expertise and élan, which in a few years, under the leadership of Franciszek Pokorny and Gwido Langer, would break the German Enigma—arguably the most impressive intellectual feat in twentieth-century cryptology. His bureau's efforts during the Russo-Polish war of 1920 demonstrated the applications of COMINT to the success of military operations. Finally, his lectures and workshops with the Japanese set that country's cryptologic efforts in a more sophisticated direction, leading to the legacy of codes and cipher systems that so challenged American cryptologists in the Pacific before and during World War II.

Notes

1. For example: *The Defeat of Soviet Russia*, "British Services of Intelligence" Vol. 1, No. 5; September 28, 1950 (hereafter referred to as "BSI").
2. Konrad Syrop, *Poland: Between the Hammer and the Anvil*, London: Robert Hale 1968, p. 111.
3. Listowell, Countess of, *Crusader in the Secret War*, London: Christopher Johnson 1952, p. 32.
4. Ibid., p. 32.
5. David Kahn, *Seizing the Enigma*, New York: Houghton Mifflin 1991, p. 50.
6. Wilhelm F. Flicke, *War Secrets of the Ether,* Frederick, MD: Office of Training, National Security Agency, Fort George G. Meade, 1959, p. 86.
7. Listowell, p. 34.
8. BSI, p. 6; Listowell, p. 35.
9. Listowell, p. 35.
10. Ibid., p. 35.
11. BSI, p. 10.
12. J. W. M. Chapman, "Japanese Intelligence, 1918–1945: A Suitable Case for Treatment" [in:] Chr. Andrew, J. Noakes, ed., *Intelligence and International Relations 1900–1945* [= Exeter Studies in History No. 15], Exeter: University of Exeter 1987, p.149.

13. Edward Layton (with Roger Pinneau and John Costello), *And I Was There*, New York: Morrow 1987, p. 30.
14. David Kahn, *The Codebreakers*, New York: Macmillan 1967, p. 579.
15. Listowell, p. 36.
16. Herbert O. Yardley, *American Black Chamber,* New York: New American Library 1984, p. 184. There is a discrepancy in the dates that Yardley assigned to Kowalewski's work with the Japanese. He places Kowalewski in Japan from late 1919 to early 1920, concurrent with that country's introduction of several new military and diplomatic codes and ciphers. During this time, Kowalewski was involved in the Polish-Bolshevik War. The exact reason for Yardley's earlier dating is unknown.

Appendix C

The French Contribution to the Breaking of Enigma

by Gilbert Bloch

The French contribution to the breaking of Enigma, the German ciphering machine, was confined to transmitting to the Poles and to the British German secret documents obtained by the French Service de Renseignement (SR) from a traitorous German Defense Ministry civil servant. France took no part either in the Polish cryptological work that led, at the end of 1932, to Enigma being reproduced and the first decrypting carried out with the reconstituted machine, or in the studies undertaken by British cryptologists from 1936 on.

But as the Polish mathematician Marian Rejewski, who was responsible for his country's success in 1932, expressly recognized, the documents provided by the French were "decisive."[1] Furthermore—and this is a question that until now has never been studied—the documents that the French continued to supply until the end of 1938 may have played a role in sustaining the Polish success. It was on the documents provided by the French that British specialists based the studies they carried out between 1936 and 1939. And lastly, it was on a French initiative that the Polish, British, and French experts met for the first time in January 1939.

The French contribution, therefore, while (1) minor, in that all the real cryptological work was done in Poland and England, was also (2) major, in that this work could not have been undertaken at all— let alone successfully—without the documents supplied by the French.

The French Contribution to Rejewski's Breakthrough in 1932

At the end of October 1930, a "Section D" was set up within the French Service de Renseignement. Its assignment was to gather by all means, fair or foul (and usually foul), information on the ciphering methods used by foreign countries. Section D had no decrypting role. It simply collected information for investigation and use by the specialists of the Service du Chiffre (which did not belong to the "Service de Renseignement" but was part of the General Staff). The man appointed as head of Section D, Capt. Gustave Bertrand, was therefore not a cryptologist, although for a short time, between 1929 and 1930, he was posted to the Service du Chiffre.

As head of Section D, Bertrand began to contact Allied countries' sister "Services." In March 1931 in Warsaw, he met with Maj. Gwido Langer, head of the Polish Biuro Szyfrów (Cipher Service) and Capt. Maksymilian Ciężki, head of its German Section (BS4).

On 1 November 1931 in Verviers, Belgium, a civil servant working for the German Ministry of Defense (Reichwehrministerium) Cipher Service (Chiffrierstelle) liaised with a French SR "middleman" (Lemoine, alias "Rex," whose real name was Rodolphe Stallman). In June and July, the German had offered to pass secret documents to the French Services. Agreement was reached at this meeting on the first, and Hans Thilo Schmidt—better known under his code names "HE" and "Asché" returned to Verviers the following Sunday, 8 November. This time, Bertrand went with Lemoine, and Asché gave him a first batch of secret documents, the most important of which were:

1. *Gebrauchsanleitung fur die Chiffriermaschine Enigma* (the Enigma ciphering machine manual), and

2. *Schlüsselanleitung zur Chiffriermaschine Enigma* (procedures for utilization of the Enigma ciphering machine).

These were instruction manuals for the German Enigma operators. They described in detail the military Enigma Type I (which had come into service on 1 June 1930) and the procedures for its use. They did not reveal the machine's internal wirings (of each rotor, of the reflector drum, and linking the different parts of the machine). These wirings were a closely guarded secret, inaccessible to Asché.

In accordance with his Section's rules, Bertrand handed the manuals over to the Service du Chiffre, which returned them on 20 November, pronouncing them to be unusable. The speed with which this damning verdict was arrived at shows that inspection must have been perfunctory, perhaps because Bertrand's relations with his former service were less than cordial.

Bertrand himself was not qualified to disagree with the specialists' opinion. But he took a step that was to be of paramount importance and was to earn him a well-deserved place in history. He asked his superiors for permission to submit the Asché documents to Allied countries' cipher services for joint study and use. That permission was duly granted.

Would the foreign specialists accept the offer and—if so would their cooperation lead to success? Bertrand must have been doubtful, but he thought that, in any case, demonstrating the SR's ability to obtain such secret material could not but enhance the Service's prestige.

Bertrand's first approach failed. Copies of the Asché documents were given to the representative in Paris of the British Intelligence Service, Comm. Wilfred Dunderdale, who took them to London on 23 November and was back in Paris on the twenty-sixth, with a flat refusal from the British authorities.

Here again, the study of the documents had been perfunctory. But the main reasons for the refusal were political. In 1931, Germany was not considered by the United Kingdom to be a threat. On the other hand, the British were suspicious of France and, in any case, mainly interested in Empire problems. There was another factor, too. The British Cipher Service (the Government Code and Cipher School) "did not think the documents sufficiently worthwhile to justify helping Bertrand to meet the costs."[2]

Disappointed by the British, Bertrand turned to the Poles. He took his documents himself to Warsaw, where Langer and Ciężki gave him an enthusiastic welcome.

The Poles had been trying to understand the new German ciphering methods since 1928.[3] They had rightly concluded that the Germans were using a machine derived from the commercial Enigma. They had noticed that the first six letters of each ciphered message showed special features and were probably some sort of key. But they had been unable to make any further progress. They could not discover the modifications that the German technicians had made to the commercial Enigma in order to transform it into the "military" type. The way the new machine was constructed and the procedures for its use remained a mystery. By 1931, the Poles had as good as given up hope of solving that mystery, and had abandoned their investigations.

Langer and Ciężki at once saw in the documents brought by Bertrand the chance to resume those investigations and bring them to a successful conclusion. Langer and Bertrand (whose respective code names were "Luc" and "Bolek") agreed to cooperate closely, dividing the task between them. In return for the documents (and for any others to be handed over in the future), the Poles would share with Bertrand all the findings they obtained.

The next few months were disappointing. However hard they tried, the team of military experts under Captain Ciężki could not reconstitute the internal wirings of the military version of Enigma. This lack of success persisted, despite the reception of more Asché documents, given to Bertrand at two meetings in Verviers on 29–30 December 1931, and 8 May 1932. These included several monthly lists of the daily settings to be used for Enigma. Bertrand took this latest information to Warsaw himself on 9 May. The Poles went on with their work, but to no avail.

In desperation, Langer and Ciężki took what must have appeared at the time to be an heroic decision. They resolved to try *civilian* experts. This move was not entirely improvised. Langer and Ciężki had thought for a long time that the mathematical skills required for cryptological studies were beyond those possessed by their military personnel. In 1929, they had organized a special course on cryptology at Poznań University for students who already had extensive mathematical knowledge. Three of the students who attended the course, Marian Rejewski,

Henryk Zygalski, and Jerzy Różycki, proved to be especially gifted. Rejewski graduated in mathematics on 1 March 1929, went for a year to the University of Göttingen in Germany, and came back to Poznań University in the summer of 1930 as an Assistant. There he joined Różycki and Zygalski in working a few hours each day in an Annex installed in Poznań by the Biuro Szyfrów. There was no mention of Enigma.

At the beginning of 1932, the three mathematicians were told that the Poznań Annex was to be closed. On 1 September, they were officially appointed to the Biuro Szyfrów in Warsaw, and spent that month studying—and decrypting—a German naval code. Then, probably in mid-October, Ciężki told Rejewski that he was to work—alone and in complete secrecy—on a new problem: trying to reconstitute the German military Enigma. Rejewski was given:

1. the two basic documents, *Gebrauchsanleitung* and *Schlüsselan-leitung* brought by Bertrand on 7 December 1931;

2. a commercial Enigma; and

3. all the German messages ciphered by Enigma, that were continually being intercepted by the Polish wireless stations set up for that purpose.

By studying the two documents given by Bertrand, Rejewski soon worked out the machine's structure and the procedures for its use.

The *Schlüsselanleitung* revealed the significance of the first six letters of each message. For each message, the Germans had to choose a three-letter key. This group of three letters determined the initial position of the three Enigma rotors as the ciphering of the message began. The three-letter key was itself ciphered, using a "basic position" (*Gründstellung*) of the rotors, which remained the same for all messages sent on a given day. So that errors could be quickly detected, the three-letter group was repeated *twice,* and the corresponding six ciphered letters put at the beginning of the message, before the text of the message itself.

Rejewski, concentrating on these first six letters, found that in 76 percent of all cases (20 out of 26) the ciphering of the six letters involved the rotation of only *one* rotor, on the far right-hand side. This meant that all the other parts of the machine could be treated as a fixed whole. Besides this, it was known that in the ciphered text the first and fourth, second and fifth and third and sixth letters were obtained by typing *the same letter* on the entry keyboard.

From these two observations Rejewski inferred the mathematical consequences. The ciphering of the six letters could be expressed by six successive permutation equations. If he had enough messages dispatched on the same day to work on (i.e., messages using the same basic position), he could discover some of the characteristics of the permutation equations. Thus the system of the six permutation equations could be "determined" in the mathematical sense of the word. It then became *theoretically* possible to solve the equations and to reconstitute the internal wirings of the right-hand Enigma rotor.

As the Germans changed the rotor order periodically, each of the three rotors in turn was located on the right-hand side of the machine. It was thus possible to deduce the internal wirings of each of the three rotors. Once this had been done, it would become possible to reconstitute the internal wirings of the reflector.

In theory, the method described above was feasible even if the machine setting was completely unknown. But in practice it was impossible. In 1932, there were no computers to handle the enormous amount of calculations involved.

Rejewski explained his reasoning to Ciężki, who was impressed by Rejewski's mathematical brilliance and gave him, on or around 15 November 1932, two further documents obtained from Asché and brought to Warsaw by Bertrand on another visit on 17–21 September. These gave the listings of the daily Enigma settings for the months of September and October. Knowing these settings, Rejewski could "simplify" his equations and so solve them.

At the time, the Germans changed the rotor order quarterly. As September and October were each in a different quarter, the internal wirings of two rotors could be reconstituted. Once these wirings were known, it became possible to reconstitute those of the third rotor and thereafter those of the fixed reflector. So it seemed that the reconstitution of the whole machine was at hand.

Rejewski's first attempts nevertheless proved vain. Thinking the matter over, Rejewski, through an astonishing mixture of mathematical brilliance and good luck, "guessed" that the Germans had made yet another change in order to transform the commercial Enigma into the military model, by linking the keys of the entry keyboard to the entry drum in alphabetical order instead of in the keyboard order. Once he had taken this final modification into account, Rejewski had no difficulty in reconstituting the machine's internal wirings. At the end of 1932, after only ten weeks' work (from 15 October to 31 December), he had succeeded.

Rejewski deserves full credit for this extraordinary achievement. It in no way detracts from that achievement to stress—as he himself did—the essential role of the four Asché documents placed at his disposal. The first two documents gave Rejewski the basis for his reasoning, the other two enabled him to solve the mathematical relations he had established. Clearly he could never have succeeded without the documents, all of them supplied by Bertrand.

Did the French Contribution Play a Role in the Polish Successes in 1933–38?

From 1933 until the end of 1938, the Poles read most of the German Army messages ciphered on Enigma and then radioed. This success continued in spite of the many changes made by the Germans to their machine and to the procedures for its use. The Poles—or, to be exact, the three mathematicians Rejewski, Zygalski, and Różycki—worked out clever techniques and produced outstandingly ingenious mechanical and electromechanical devices. Only at the end of 1938, following further modifications by the Germans, were the Poles no longer able to penetrate the Enigma traffic.

The French contribution to the Polish success in 1932 is widely acknowledged, though often underestimated. But for the years 1933–38, no mention of a French contribution is made. Does this silence reflect reality?

The Polish mathematicians always said that no secret German documents other than the four given to Rejewski during the fourth quarter of 1932 were ever put at their disposal. Rejewski, in particular, had to answer questions on this point many times, and his replies never varied. There is no reason to doubt his sincerity or the exactitude of his statements. He certainly told the truth. It was only in 1939, in fact, that Rejewski and his colleagues learned that the four documents had been supplied by Bertrand.

On the other hand, there is no doubt at all that, through Asché, the French SR went on receiving, from November 1931 until August 1938, a great number of German secret documents referring to Enigma; and it is equally certain that Bertrand passed all these documents on, very quickly, to Langer and Ciężki. In his book *Enigma*, on page 32, Bertrand states that besides the *Gebrauchsanleitung* and the *Schlüsselanleitung* Asché supplied *all* the monthly lists of Enigma daily settings over the period December 1931–June 1934 and ten other important documents as well. We know, moreover, that contrary to what Bertrand seems to infer in his book, the flow of Enigma documents did not dry up after June 1934. True, Asché was transferred that year from the Chiffrierstelle to the Forschungsamt [Research Bureau]. But he was still attached administratively to the Chiffrierstelle and was if anything even better placed than before to obtain cryptological documents—particularly on Enigma—and give them to the French SR. In his book, *"Notre espion chez Hitler,"* Colonel Paillole states that *twenty-three* monthly lists of daily Enigma settings were handed over by Asché over the period July 1934–September 1938 and passed on to the Poles. Besides these monthly lists, it seems highly probable that Asché supplied details of the changes the Germans made to the machine and to procedures. Between 1931 and 1939, Bertrand traveled to Warsaw thirteen times, and Langer (perhaps accompanied by Ciężki) came to Paris just as often. Bertrand never went to Warsaw empty-handed, nor did

Langer ever go home empty-handed. Each time the men met, information and documents were handed over by the French to the Poles. Undeniably, Langer and Ciężki received many, many documents. But those documents were never shown to the mathematicians working in their service.

So two questions have to be answered:

1. Why, apart from the four manuals used by Rejewski in 1932, did Langer and Ciężki not give their mathematicians any of the data made available by the French SR?

2. Did those data, although not given to the Polish mathematicians, nevertheless help the Poles with their decrypting?

The first question is easily answered. Every Service keeps to the "need-to-know" rule. Each agent is given only the information absolutely indispensable for his own work. If war broke out, Langer and Ciężki wanted to be able to decrypt the German messages without outside help. Once Rejewski had made his breakthrough at the end of 1932, the Polish mathematicians were able to determine *by themselves* the Enigma daily settings and each message key, and to decrypt the messages. It was therefore quite normal to let them do so (the Asché documents could be used to check their work). The heads of the Biuro Szyfrów had no reason to disclose to their subordinates the existence of other sources of information. That might even have made the mathematicians feel that their work was of no value.

Answering the second question raises more complex problems. Between the beginning of 1933 and the end of 1938, the Germans twice modified their machine. On 1 November 1937, they replaced the original reflector (*Umkehrwalze A*) by another one (*Umkehrwalze B*). On 15 December 1938, they added to the set of three rotors (I, II, and III) used previously two new rotors (IV and V), thus increasing the number of possible settings of the rotors from 6 to 60.

Besides, the Germans made many modifications to their procedures during that period. They increased the frequency of the changes in the setting of the various parts of the machine; they increased the number of elements to be changed; and they made basic alterations in their procedures.

1. At the beginning of 1933, the rotor order was modified only quarterly. From 1 January 1936, onwards it was changed monthly, and from 1 October, daily.

2. At the beginning of 1933, the number of rotors (*Steckers*) in daily use was six. After 1 October 1936, the number varied (five to eight); at the end of 1938 it was set at ten.

3. On 15 September 1938, the procedure of setting a basic position (*Grundstellung*) for all messages on a given day was discontinued. Thenceforward the operator had to choose a different basic position for each message.

Faced with these many changes, the Poles reacted efficiently—and with amazing speed—every time. On each occasion decrypting seems to have been interrupted for only a very short time, or even not at all. Until 15 December 1938, the Poles were able to go on reading the German messages.

The Polish mathematicians, because they had worked out the mathematical theory of the machine and had practical experience too, were perfectly capable of overcoming the new difficulties raised by each change. But beforehand, it was essential to arrive at a precise "diagnosis," i.e., to identify exactly what changes had been made. It may seem strange that it was possible to make such an accurate and immediate diagnosis in every case. Could the documents and information supplied by Bertrand provide a—partial—explanation?

In some cases, the changes made (for instance, in the number of *Steckers* to be used daily) could be identified easily and quickly by studying the texts of the intercepted messages. But in others that explanation is less plausible, and the Poles themselves have given other reasons. According to the Poles, for instance, when the Germans replaced the Enigma reflector on 1 November 1937, they sent a ciphered message in advance to all Enigma operators, reminding them of the nature and time of the change, and that message, intercepted and decrypted by the Poles, put the latter on the right track. Similarly, the existence of rotors IV and V was said to have been known, through Intelligence, long before they were put into service, because the rotors were distributed to the units a long time ahead. All these explanations are plausible. However, without calling the Polish achievement into question, another theory may be put forward.

For instance, the monthly lists of daily Enigma settings to be used for the months of January–February and October 1936 (handed by Asché to Bertrand on 24 January and 14 October, respectively, and probably quickly passed on to the Poles) made it clear that the rotor order was to be modified more often and the number of *Steckers* used daily changed. Had the Polish mathematicians not been able to identify the nature of the changes, Langer and Ciężki would have been in a position to point their research in the right direction, telling them that their information came from some other source. In the cases mentioned, it seems unlikely that they had to intervene. The mathematicians could easily have identified the changes by studying the intercepted messages themselves. But other changes lead to trickier questions.

As regards the replacement of Reflector A by Reflector B on 1 November 1937, Bertrand could have tipped off the Poles, though this is merely a hypothesis. Asché, who was surely aware of the change, met the SR representatives on 6 and 15 November. It is possible that he warned them.

Much more puzzling are the events of the last four months of 1938. On 15 September, the Enigma operators abandoned the basic position (*Grundstellung*) procedure previously utilized for all messages on a given day. On 15 December, Rotors IV and V were put into service. Furthermore, on an unconfirmed date (perhaps 1 January 1939), the number of *Steckers* to be used daily was raised to ten. A study of the messages intercepted could not readily have led to a clear identification of any of these modifications. Yet here again the Poles were able to get their diagnosis right every time.

That the basic position was to be abandoned for 15 September on was evident from the monthly list of daily Enigma configurations for

September 1938 given by Asché to the French SR as early as 9 August. That list was in fact *the last one* Asché ever gave. He brought it to Paris, where he stayed from 9–11 August. It seems very likely that at the same time Asché gave Bertrand a copy of the new German instructions (*Deckblatter No. 1 bis 13*). These instructions not only indicated that the basic position was to be abandoned, but mentioned that ten *Steckers* were to be used each day "as soon as the necessary number of *Steckers* could be made available to all units." Furthermore at the time of his stay in Paris Asché certainly knew that in the near future (he may not have been aware of the exact date) Rotors IV and V were to be brought into service. Here again it is very likely that he told Bertrand this. We can be sure that Bertrand learned a great deal from Asché in the course of the latter's stay in Paris, simply because almost immediately after his visitor's departure Bertrand set off again to Warsaw, staying there from 22–27 August. So all the data brought by Asché to Paris was almost immediately afterwards placed in the hands of the Poles. Langer and Ciężki knew what modifications the Germans were planning, and so could put the mathematicians on the right track.

As soon as Rotors IV and V were brought into service, the Poles were able to reproduce them. On the other hand, they could not at short notice multiply their equipment and their personnel by ten and so, after 15 December, they ceased to be able to decrypt the German messages.

The theory set out above, i.e., that the Poles probably did make use of the documents and information supplied by Asché and passed on to them by Bertrand seems to be borne out by the course of events after 1 January 1939. During his visit to Paris, Asché had handed over information covering the period up through December 1938. But that was the last time that he was to deliver intelligence on Enigma. Strikingly, the Poles, who up to then had been able to pinpoint all the modifications made in the Enigma machine and the procedures for its use, found themselves at a loss from 1 January onwards. They thought, mistakenly, that besides increasing the number of *Steckers* to ten the Germans had made *other* changes on 1 January. In fact, the Germans had made no other changes, as the Bletchley Park studies carried out during the last quarter of 1939 made clear.

To sum up, Bertrand passed on documents and information to Langer and Ciężki from 1933 until 1938. There is no doubt at all about that. That those documents and information played a role cannot be proved, and the theories put forward here are only theories. But they cannot be dismissed. Even if in fact they reflect reality, that would not take away from the merit of the work done by the Poles. They alone attempted to reconstitute and decrypt the Enigma—and they succeeded. But it does seem likely that they had more help than has hitherto been thought.

THE FRENCH CONTRIBUTION TO THE BRITISH STUDIES (1936–38)

In November 1931, the British had refused to cooperate with Bertrand. Nevertheless, they had carefully filed away the copies of the *Gebrauchsanleitung* and the *Schlüsselanleitung* he had brought them. Hitler's seizure of power and his rearmament policy led the British to change their minds about Germany and events there—including the new ciphering methods—were no longer a matter of indifference. In 1936, the Asché documents of 1931 were carefully studied.

The French SR was contacted in 1936 and 1938, and Bertrand gave the GCCS at least some of the documents he possessed including (in 1938) "the plain and cipher texts of four Army Enigma messages with the plugboard connections and settings used."[4] This is worth mentioning here because it shows quite clearly that Asché handed over much more than basic documents and monthly lists of Enigma settings. Although no mention could be found in GCCS records (which "are far from perfect for the prewar years"[5]), it is reasonably certain that monthly lists of Enigma settings also reached the British cryptologists who had begun to work on Enigma in 1936. Thanks to the data supplied by Bertrand, they were by then in the same position as the Poles in 1932. Their mathematical abilities (and particularly those of Alfred Dillwyn Knox) were equal to Rejewski's, and they reasoned along the same lines. But they did not guess (as Rejewski had) the final modification the Germans had made to the commercial Enigma. Miracles can happen only once!

Nevertheless, the British efforts were not a dead loss—far from it. Their cryptologists' familiarity with Enigma's structure and the procedures for its use was to pay handsome dividends after the Poles made them the gift of a reconstituted Enigma machine in July 1939. The British were able to start work on it at once, so obviating several months' apprenticeship.

A French Initiative: The First Meeting in Paris of the Polish, British, and French Cryptologists

Towards the end of 1938, Bertrand was becoming impatient. He had been supplying information to the Poles for seven years and to the British for three. Apart from polite thanks, he had received nothing in exchange. The Poles, despite their promises in 1931, had kept their achievements strictly secret. The British had not been able to reconstitute the Enigma. The Enigma effort had apparently been a total failure. Moreover, it had cost the French SR dearly. The huge sums of money paid to Asché had sorely taxed the SR's limited resources, and the investment seemed to have been made in vain.

The British and the Poles were working separately, with no contact. Bertrand thought it might be valuable to hold a meeting of all the experts so that they could report what progress they had made. He seems to have had great difficulty in persuading the British to agree to such a meeting. In the end, he obtained Denniston's agreement, and on 8–9 January 1939, the Polish, British and French experts met for the first time and sat around the same table.

Apparently, the meeting achieved little. Langer and Ciężki had been forbidden by their superiors to reveal any of their successes (or their difficulties) unless the other participants showed that they, too, had obtained comparable results. The British (Denniston and Knox) could only say they had found it impossible to reconstitute the machine. The French (Bertrand and the cryptologist Captain Braquenie) had nothing to offer. The experts got to know each other, wined and dined together at Drouant (at the SR's expense!) and parted with a promise to meet again if there were any new developments.

In fact, this first contact did turn out to have been useful. When the United Kingdom, in March 1939, gave a solemn undertaking to Poland to come to its assistance in case of need, the certainty that war was inevitable was a spur to closer cooperation. This time the Poles took the initiative and convened another meeting in Warsaw on 25 July 1939. At that meeting they shared with their allies all the knowledge they had gained through eight years' work. The results of this Polish gift are well known today.

Bertrand was rewarded for all the information he had supplied for eight years by being informed by the Poles of the revelation to be made at the Warsaw meeting . . . one day before it took place. He also had the satisfaction of escorting personally to London the Polish replica of Enigma intended for the British, which he presented to Menzies on 16 August 1939. Small reward indeed!

Many years later, Bertrand decided to write a book revealing his role. Published in 1973, *Enigma, ou la plus grande énigme de la Guerre 1939–1945* was far from perfect, and only a few copies were sold. But it did have the historical merit of ending the absolute secrecy observed until then on the Enigma story. It was Bertrand's book that started the flow of publications and disclosures thanks to which we now know what happened.

History—and historians—owe a good deal to Bertrand and his Service.

Notes

1. Marian Rejewski, "How the Polish mathematicians broke Enigma" (English translation of an article published in *Wiadomości matematyczne*, 1980, 1–28), [in:] W. Kozaczuk, *Enigma,* English edition

1984. Page 258: "Hence, the conclusion is that the intelligence material furnished to us should be regarded as having been decisive to solution of the machine. A number of years later, I learned that the material had been supplied by the aforementioned Captain (later General) Bertrand."

2. F. H. Hinsley et al., *British Intelligence in the Second World War,* Vol. 3, Part 2, p. 947.

3. A first machine, derived from the commercial Enigma slightly modified, had been adopted by the German navy in February 1926. The German army followed in July 1928 with another adaptation of the commercial Enigma. The military Enigma proper was brought into service on 1 June 1930.

4. F. H. Hinsley et al., op. cit., Vol. 3, Part 2, p. 950.

5. F. H. Hinsley et al., op. cit., Vol. 1, p. 488.

Appendix D

A New Challenge for an Old Enigma-Buster

by Władysław Kozaczuk

Cryptologia, July 1990, Volume XIV Number 3

In the summer of 1976, Marian Rejewski, Polish mathematician-cryptologist, the solver of the German Enigma cipher, was sent, by a former signals office from England, a letter including a photocopy of an enciphered message, dated 26 April 1904. This was the period of the Russo-Japanese War. The piece was a correspondence between the Polish Socialist Party (of which Józef Piłsudski was a leader) and its emissaries in London. Despite his advanced age and a prolonged ailment, and contrary to his initial objections, Rejewski solved the cipher, which turned out to reveal an interesting historical document. The story I wish now to recount, poring over old but only recently acquired documents about Enigma, happened in the mid-1970s, when heated discussions in newspapers and learned debates of historians over two sensational books[1] were at their peak.

By 1976, in Poland's capital, a kind of "hotline" existed between the seventy-one-year-old Marian Rejewski, the mathematician-cryptologist who had just become world famous as the solver of the German Enigma machine cipher, and myself, a historian who strove to keep pace with the burgeoning mass of publications on Enigma, some enlightening but many inaccurate.

So it was not unusual that on that sunny summer afternoon of 17 August 1976, having been summoned by a call from the other end of the line, I jumped into my old German Wartburg to speed through the crowded streets of central Warsaw to the northern district of Zolibórz ("Joli Bord," or "Beautiful Shore") where Rejewski and his family lived.

Just as we were about to immerse ourselves in the reading of newly received correspondence from West and East Germany, Sweden, Belgium, France, or Brazil, the doorbell rang and Rejewski's seven-year-old grandson Wojtek brought in a small, inconspicuous letter; he was a keen collector of postage stamps and was always the first to greet the postman with a polite "Good morning." This time Wojtek was disappointed: the envelope bore only a small olive gray stamp with an image of Britain's Queen Elizabeth II, with her familiar refined profile.

The letter, dated 10 August 1976, was from one of Rejewski's permanent correspondents, Tadeusz Lisicki, a Polish World War II signals officer and former commander of a radio-communications center located at Boxmoor in Greater London, where Rejewski and other Polish cryptologists, who had escaped in 1943 from German-occupied southern France, had resumed work on cracking Nazi ciphers almost to the end of the war. In fact it was only after he and fellow codebreaker, Henryk Zygalski (nearly as brilliant as he), had in August 1943 reached the British Isles and been installed at Boxmoor that mass reading of German SS, Gestapo, and Himmler's other secret radio traffic had started.

Since the start of the war, the British had enormously enlarged their decryption center at Bletchley, some fifty miles northwest of London, where more than nine thousand cryptologists, technicians, and intelligence officers were busy solving, translating, analyzing, and passing to Allied field commands hundreds of thousands of German, Italian, and other Axis military and political radio messages. But Rejewski and Zygalski never saw Bletchley: they only learned of its existence thirty years later, when in 1973 and 1974, respectively, Bertrand's and Winterbotham's books about the Allies' "most secret source," as Winston Churchill called it, revealed it and opened the subject of Allied cryptanalysis to more comprehensive study.

As of this date, two dozen books and innumerable scholarly papers have been published on various aspects of Enigma and Ultra in Britain, Poland, the U.S., France, Germany, Italy, Yugoslavia, Belgium and other countries.

The letter from Lisicki included three sheets of paper, darkened and streaked from poor photocopying. It took close scrutiny to discern the numerals and letters of a handwritten cryptogram. The date of its composition was the easiest thing to establish: at the top of the first page, in plain text, was the date 24.IV.1904, [24 April 1904]. There were also several unenciphered words, including some Polish first and last names. It was one of eighty enciphered messages between the Polish Socialist Party and its emissaries in London, now held in the Piłsudski Institute in New York.

This letter had been written in the period of the Russo-Japanese War, which had begun on 8 February 1904, and the name—actually a pseudonym—"Mieczysław" stood for none other than the Polish Socialist and future head of independent Poland, Józef Piłsudski, who in 1904 was staying in Austrian-governed Cracow. Another pseudonym, "Karski," stood for Piłsudski's closest aide and emissary to London, Tytus Filipowicz. In the spring of 1904, Piłsudski and several colleagues were trying to reach an agreement with the Japanese diplomatic representatives in Britain, and through them with the Japanese government in Tokyo.

Why negotiations between the Poles, then partly under Russian and partly under German rule, and the Land of the Rising Sun?

The Poles hoped to receive Japanese support on the international scene for the restoration of an independent Poland. Piłsudski's Polish Socialist Party also sought to obtain from the Japanese modern rifles, together with substantial stocks of ammunition. In return, the Poles would divert the Czarist armies with a rising of underground forces and would provide intelligence on the Russian order of battle and troop movements. The prospects for this seemed more realistic since the spring, when reports from Manchuria suggested the eventual defeat of the Czarist armies. A more practical near objective of the Poles was to obtain better treatment for the Poles drafted into the Russian army who had been captured by the Japanese and were being held in atrocious conditions in Japan's Manchurian prisoner-of-war camps.

It seemed doubtful, however, whether these historical facts would be helpful in attempting to decrypt the ciphers. Rejewski was not at all pleased to have received them.

"The enclosures to your letter," wrote Rejewski in his reply, "are truly a gift of the Danae. I feel a very strong temptation to start work on them but, at the same time, I do not want to do so since this is not my field, nor is it for my age and condition of health. I have, nevertheless, taken a closer look at them. That this is an encipherment procedure in which three different keys are used is no real discovery, as this can easily be guessed from the several words given in plain language, and not only from the different frequencies of cipher groups. To be sure, there are many repetitions, but they are too short for a simple cipher [as a rule, they comprise only two groups each]. The brevity of the repetitions could be explained, for instance, by the fact that, as substitutes for certain common letters, several different symbols were used, or that the symbols represent certain digraphs, such as *ch, cz, sz,* certain short words such as *nie* ["no" or "not"], or numerals or punctuation marks.

"But one may also attempt to explain the brevity of the repetitions by other hypotheses, for instance, that the cipher has been peppered with meaningless 'null' groups of numerals, etc. But if one wished to study all this, hc would have to prepare operational sheets on which he could freely mark with zigzags, flourishes, etc., using variously colored pencils. All that would be rather difficult to manage, however, since some of the cipher groups are illegible, and the middle page has been photocopied so badly that part of the cipher text has been cut off.

"The essence of the matter, however, is that I am reluctant to undertake this job, particularly in this season of the year: it is the end of August, and soon it will be my favorite month, September; we will have our golden Polish autumn and under the circumstances I have no desire to pore over ciphers in a closed room. Maybe in the winter I'll set to work on it, but I wouldn't like to make any promises."

Rejewski's reluctance to attack the cipher was no doubt caused mainly by his declining health and by his plans to vacation, as usual, during the "golden Polish autumn." He had not yet completely recovered from the emotional aftereffects of a sudden loss of consciousness, during the night of 5–6 March 1976, after which he had been hospitalized for several weeks in the Neuropsychiatric Clinic in southern Warsaw. After Rejewski had returned home, his wife Irena used to phone me, unbeknownst to her husband, when she became alarmed at the strenuous demands that he placed on himself or at the exhausting visits of swarms of press, radio and TV reporters and interviewers, of second- and third-rate writers and of other sensation-mongers. To keep them at bay was not easy even with the joint efforts of Mrs. Rejewska and myself.

In mid-August 1976, a few days after her husband had received the letter in question, a phone call from Irena dealt for a change not with such intruders. She was concerned about her husband's "suspicious" behavior. Did I have any idea as to the cause of his restlessness and excitement? Could it have some connection with the letter that he had received from Britain?

During my last meeting with Rejewski, he had shown a noticeable lack of interest in the letter with the cipher. Why should he now be agitated or excited, pacing, as his wife told me, back and forth in his room, muttering to himself something that she could not understand? And why should he have mentioned to her on two or three occasions that he would rather stay home while she and Wojtek took a vacation out of town?

But it would be a difficult task to try to convince Rejewski to take better care of his health and to go along with his wife's wish to detach him from strenuous, if voluntary, mental labors, at least during that year's golden September. His evident gentleness, his refined manners and self-possession in speech and behavior, with glimpses of subtle irony and dry humor that tended to self-deprecation, but without any tendency to hurt others or to diminish the achievements of his two mathematician-colleagues who had been involved in cracking Enigma—all these traits only camouflaged his quiet yet adamant will. Hence, I hesitated to invade his world of thoughts and decisions. Perhaps it really would be better for him to spend his beloved September not in a noisy spa on the Baltic coast, but in his quiet district of Warsaw, after his family had left, and having plenty of time for quiet walks in the nearby Bielany Park, decked out in its autumnal colors. It was in the same Bielany Park where he used to walk almost every weekend until September 1939, when he went to war, continuing his own war of wits with the Nazis which had begun seven years earlier, when he had begun work on Germany's Enigma ciphers.

Neither was I, for that matter, planning to leave Warsaw for a September vacation that year. Hence, I was far from taken aback when I got a phone call asking me urgently to come and "discuss a number of matters that have just cropped up." I gave in immediately, as it has become my custom since 1973, when Enigma began to play havoc with my life and with the established history of the Second World War, revealing many new angles and hitherto unknown aspects. In a word, I called the same afternoon at Rejewski's apartment.

This time Rejewski was not his usual controlled self. He had dropped his manner of carefully guarding his state of mind and emotions and he was evidently elated.

Since 1973, it had become Rejewski's custom to pass me carbon or cyclostyled copies of practically all the papers he wrote as well as the comments and remarks he made on books and other publications concerning Enigma or cryptology. This was also true of copies of those documents that he thought might be used by researchers dealing with the history of Enigma and of cryptology. That was why I had been called in that day.

My appearance in his apartment resulted in his brusquely waving a single sheet of paper at me, which, he said shortly, was the fruit of a month of efforts to break and convert into intelligible language an arcane handwritten cipher dating back to the 1904 Russo-Japanese War. Though his voice was calm and impassive when he handed the text to me, I could see his delight on his face. I refrained from pushing him into replying to the questions I wanted to ask, leaving him to venture his comments when he thought fit. After all, he had clearly done the job despite his own earlier and forcefully expressed objections.

So I got down to scrutinizing the contents of that sheet of paper and as I did I became increasingly absorbed by what I encountered. For this was a fascinating display of a brilliant mind at work, sensible words and whole sentences extracted by the codebreaker's alchemy from the seemingly meaningless raw material of the indistinct rows of figures on the three pages presented to me one month earlier.

Rejewski had cryptanalyzed the text and the translation appears below:

Grzegorz [Gregory]

26 April 1904

Dear Friend,
Part I enciphered with our usual key.
Part II: Bystrzycki, Part III with the Bolek and Mieczysław key. Karski told me it exists only in our yard (the Intelligence Bureau). It was then proposed 90 to 93 (i.e., for 3 points).

The requirements set for what is in parentheses above are as follows: Kharkov Moscow Siberia, one special agent for each AN. EO of the Army Corps mobilization, the number of transferred troops, their time of departure.

Kharkov, it is known that the first four Army C[orps] are in Manchuria. It is confidentially known that the 17th will be or has been mobilized [and] will depart in early May. The next to go will be the 10th Army Corps, stationed in Kursk and [Kharkov?] in July. Obtain information concerning strength and composition and check whether and where it is to go.

II. Moscow: Information required on each regiment passing through, where it is going and by what route. Siberia: how many trains go every day, the number of men and the quantities of ammunition and food; also when the circular road around Lake Baikal will be opened, the same [. . .] to it.

III. Exact description of the Baltic Fleet and when it is to go East. The number of men and artillery dispatched to the war in Manchuria in the second half of last year and in the first and second halves of the present year.

Dear Friends,
    What was promised has been done. The friend [. . .] reports that his friend + who lives near his wife [?] is ready to do all that is required but in return for this affair he is asking for almost double the amount envisioned in today's conversation.
+ Colonel
It has been late. Greetings SK (the last key!)

    I do not think that Rejewski really cared about the meaning hidden in those deciphered rows of digits. He was very far from being any kind of a *homo historicus* or *homo politicus*. To the historian interested in that specific period, however, this text was no minor find.
    On 2 June 1904, two and a half months after the message had been written, Piłsudski turned up in London, where he met the Japanese ambassador, Hayashi, several times. The result was an invitation to visit Tokyo. On 11 June, Piłsudski arrived by ship in New York accompanied by Tytus Filipowicz (later Polish ambassador to the United States) and on 21 June, he arrived by train in San Francisco. The next day he embarked on the SS *Coptic* for Japan, arriving there on 10 July.
    In the end, Piłsudski's political negotiations in Tokyo had little practical consequence. But he did gain one thing: the Japanese military command agreed to substantially facilitate the purchase of weapons and ammunition and issued appropriate instructions to that effect to Japanese military attachés in several European countries.
    I am more than convinced that Rejewski's solution did not come like a bolt of genius out of the blue—unlike a significant portion of his solution of the Enigma. That is clear from the number of auxiliary cryptological tables that reveal some of the secrets of his intellectual workshop. And if a moment of illumination did arrive, it had to be supported and developed with his patient perseverance, the endless, painstaking toil which is the classical cryptologist's lot. With this in mind, someone not acquainted with the manner in which Rejewski expressed his

thoughts and feelings, the way in which he played down his efforts and the results they bring, would surely be misled by taking literally the wording of the letter he sent the same day, 17 September 1976, to Lisicki:

"Thanks for your letters of the 29th August and 8th September 1976. They arrived almost simultaneously. I shall deal with them in a moment, but before I do, a couple of words on the 1904 cipher. In the end I did tackle it for it was giving me no rest and, additionally, seemed to offer no real problems. In effect I had no great trouble in cracking it (if it had been more difficult and time-consuming I would not have touched it). The contents of the message as I read it are presented on the enclosed separate sheet, together with the keys I used and the method applied. There should be little trouble with solving the remaining material [in the Piłsudski Institute] even if the keys used differ. I must admit that I feel some satisfaction with solving that cipher, which I might compare with the successful tackling of a difficult crossword, but I would prefer not to try to solve any more ciphers ever again: I cannot or do not want to tackle more difficult ones. As far as these specific ones are concerned, they ceased to fascinate me once I had broken them. Now I would like to get back to your letters."

He then delved into the intricacies and personalities of the Enigma solution in four densely typed pages—four of the more than one thousand in Polish, English, French, and German addressed to persons the whole world over: in France, Britain, Sweden, Germany, and Yugoslavia in Europe; to the United States and Brazil in the Western Hemisphere. The most frequently mentioned topics were the technical intricacies of the cipher machine, the wartime friendly and efficient cooperation among British, French, and Polish codebreakers and the officers who commanded the various outfits in which they served. But also there was much about the rivalries and infighting among the wartime allies, as well as lots of political and social gossip and, even tidbits bordering on libel. Truly, a treasure-trove of facts and opinions for present and future historians. A common feature can be discerned in all his letters: they are miracles of precision though marked by his own, unmistakable understatements and refined humor. One last remark on that cipher from the 1904–05 Russo-Japanese War. Rejewski cracked it in August 1976 when he was seventy-one and had been ailing for several months; the thing I possibly best remember of what he told me when I arrived that day to see and appreciate the results of his efforts was a reflective remark he uttered, looking rather absent-mindedly out of an open window towards some imaginary horizon which he alone could see.

"You know," he said "something durable can surely be expected from anyone who claims to be a cryptologist, a codebreaker. Do you agree?"

Note

1. Gustave Bertrand *Enigma, ou la plus grande énigme de la guerre 1939–1945* (Paris, 1973); F. W. Winterbotham, *The Ultra Secret* (London, 1974).

Biographical Sketch

Władysław Kozaczuk, Ph.D., a Polish historian, is the author of a number of books, including *Wehrmacht 1933–39* (a standard Polish work on German rearmament and war preparations); *Secret Battle: The Intelligence Services of Poland and the German Reich, 1922–39;* and *Enigma, The Peripheries of Hell* (concerning Switzerland's armed neutrality in World War II, published recently.)

Appendix E

A British Cryptanalyst Salutes the Polish Cryptanalysts

by Alan Stripp

I should like to pay belated tribute to the outstanding achievement of the Polish cryptanalysts in the sheer excellence of the work that they started in the 1930s. I believe that, now that the story is better known, many of my wartime colleagues, at Bletchley Park and its outstations, would join in this message.

Firstly, their work contributed directly towards our successful breaking and reading of Enigma traffic, in increasing volume and complexity, throughout the war. Secondly, it thus played an important part in helping Britain to survive the earlier years of the war, and to achieve final victory six years later.

The all-important role played by Rejewski, Różycki, Zygalski, Lisicki, and all their colleagues during that troubled period before the war is still insufficiently recognized here. Although they worked in a small unit with relatively slender resources, they were far in advance of anything that British and French cryptanalysts could then achieve. Moreover, Poland managed to convince first France and then a reluctant Britain that they were succeeding where we were failing, and that they could offer us help of immense value. To do that, when it was almost certain that Poland would soon be engulfed in the approaching German invasion, showed a generous and unselfish longsightedness which was almost unprecented, and is still not fully recognized.

Why has it taken so long for this to become at all widely known in Britain? Why were Rejewski and Zygalski, after they eventually arrived here in the summer of 1943, given no opportunity to share in the breaking of successively harder versions of Enigma which they had themselves pioneered and taught us? Setting them to work on the Doppellkassetten system was like using racehorses to pull wagons.

I cannot offer any convincing explanation for this. It is clear that of the many people who worked on Enigma at Bletchley Park (henceforth "BP") very few ever knew about the Polish contribution; the "need to know" principle extended to that as to many other matters there. The first published description of BP's work came in fragmentary and distorted form in Winterbotham's book of 1974. An account which assures us that "a bronze-colored column, surmounted by a larger circular bronze-colored face, like some Eastern Goddess" was "the oracle of Bletchley" is not likely to help us far towards the truth. Did he mean a bombe? The color suggests that.

During the next dozen years, fragments of that earlier history gradually emerged. Welchman's book, *The Hut Six Story*, published in 1982 despite intense official disapproval, said little about the Polish work. He explained that he did not know which of several stories to believe, though he does say, "The vital point is that the Poles managed to give us the details of the machine and the benefit of their experience in time for us to exploit them early in the war." Later he wrote "I had not even appreciated our debt to Rejewski until Professor Stengers sent me a copy of his paper in the February 1981 issue of *L'Histoire*." He did not hear of Garliński's book *The Enigma War* in time to use it in his own book.

Since then, there has been a growing stream of revelations—not all of them accurate—about the role of the British cryptanalysts. The stream has sometimes been dammed by official disapproval, but then the leaks have become so embarrassing that the truth has, in any case, trickled out, though still—naturally enough in Britain—with the emphasis on our successes.

In the recent book *Codebreakers: The Inside Story of Bletchley Park*, edited by Sir Harry Hinsley and myself, once again the Polish contribution is mentioned only in passing. That is easily explained: The book is specifically about the work of BP and its outstations, and it became clear at an early stage that the story, told by men and women who had worked there, would more than fill the three hundred pages agreed on. Only a few of the older contributors had ever heard of the Poles' work. In any case we had to omit other important links in the Ultra chain for the same reason: the initial interception of enemy signals, for example, and the final secure distribution of the resulting intelligence.

Yet another difficulty is that Kozaczuk's revealing book, *Enigma*, has never become widely known here, and his later *Geheim-operation Wicher* is so far available only in German—a great stumbling-block still for most English readers.

None of these obstacles was in itself insuperable; unfortunately in combination they proved formidable. I hope that this small tribute may help to make amends.

Cambridge, July 1995

Biography

Alan Stripp was recruited as a first-year student in Classics at Trinity College, Cambridge, in 1943. After an intensive course in written Japanese at Bedford, he spent six months working on the Japanese army/air force code at Bletchley Park before moving to Delhi to continue that work until the end of the war. He then spent a further year working on the Persian and Afghan diplomatic code systems (the latter, a one-man job) during the Azerbaijan crisis, and took part in a course in Russian, before returning to Cambridge.

After finishing his degree course, he worked for two years in Portugal and four in Indonesia. In 1954, he again returned to Cambridge and joined the university staff. For several years, he directed the annual courses on intelligence. He is now a self-employed lecturer and writer.

Appendix F

The Polish Success with Enigma in British Literature

by Zdzisław Jan Kapera

There was a brief but significant discussion on the Net "Intelligence Forum" in October 2001. The subject was the title of the new book *Action This Day: Bletchley Park from the Breaking of the Enigma Code to the Birth of the Modern Computer,* edited by Michael Smith and Ralph Erskine. It reminded me of a series of jokes once popular in Poland about Radio Erevan. To every question about the source of a Western technological innovation there was an answer saying that some Russian had invented the same gadget earlier. For example, that there was a Russian by the name of Popov who invented the radio five years before Marconi, and so on. Now, for the recent discussion about the title of the new British book. As soon as its publication was announced on the Net, various people commented on the choice of the subtitle. Philip H. Jacobsen wrote: "This should be an excellent book for those interested in cryptological history. However, the title seems to imply that Bletchley Park 'broke' the Enigma code. I thought that the German military Enigma machine cipher was 'broken' by the Polish mathematicians and cryptographers Marian Rejewski, Jerzy Różycki, and Henryk Zygalski in late December 1932."

Frode Weierud, who first publicized the book on the Net, had this to say in answer: "English not being my mother tongue, I am not able to judge the finer nuances of the English language, but I must admit I fail to see a problem with the *Action This Day* title." He continued, "As we all know (or should know), the Poles made the initial break into the Enigma; GCCS at Bletchley Park and OP 20 of the U.S. Navy were breaking the Enigma throughout the war." The discussion aroused the interest of Ludwig Kruh, a regular writer for the section "Reviews and Things Cryptologic" in the *Cryptologia* quarterly. He simply looked inside the book and announced, "I just checked the index and found sixteen references to 'Poland: codebreaking,' and while it is not on the cover full credit is given where it belongs."

Eventually, Ralph Erskine, one of the editors and contributors to the book (which consists of a collection of historical essays), an internationally acknowledged expert on the history of the Naval Enigma who researched the British and American archives thoroughly, defended himself in these words: "As *Action This Day* points out (p. 47), GCCS's solutions of plugboard Enigma owe much to Polish cryptanalysts, who were the first to solve it in 1932 . . . However, Enigma has a long story, and there were many different versions of Enigma . . . Chapter 4 of the book contains 'Reminiscences on Enigma' by Hugh Fox, who joined GCCS in 1924. These reveal that he devised methods to solve a version of commercial Enigma C (known to GCCS as the 'Index Model') in 1927. Although written in 1949, his 'Reminiscences' are confirmed by PRO file HW 25/14, which contains a detailed explanation, compiled at that time, of the methods he used in 1927." Mr. Erskine concluded, "It's not easy to encapsulate almost twenty years of solving Enigma in a book title" (as well as cover some of GCCS's other achievements!)

Yes, as a publisher I agree that it is not easy to devise a good title for a book. But it should certainly not be misleading, and in my opinion the subtitle of this book is misleading. Everybody knows, or should know, as Mr. Jacobsen stressed, that the military version of Enigma was broken by Rejewski at the end of 1932. This is a fact nobody can dispute, and the military Enigma is the subject of the book. However, the discussion around the book's title is significant in that it reveals a growing problem. The more we know about Enigma and the methods used to decipher it, as well as about the American contribution from

1943 on, the stronger appears to be the British tendency to diminish the role of the Poles.

The lack of proper attribution started anew with Robert Harris's *Enigma*, a war thriller published in England in 1995, in which, although mention is made of the Polish contribution, one of the characters in the story, a Polish cryptographer at Bletchley Park, is a traitor. He is about to provide the Germans with proof that the Enigma code was broken and that it was done in revenge for the British silence about the Katyń Forest massacre. Mr. Pukowski, the traitor, is a complete invention. Even though there is a note in the book saying that all characters are fictional, the text immediately preceding these words states clearly that the novel is based on historical facts and that the German messages quoted therein are all authentic. As far as I was able to check, it seems possible that some of the decoded texts in the book are authentic, especially those connected with the Naval Enigma code "Shark." However, I am sure that the German reports on the Katyń Forest massacre are invented by Harris. Had they been authentic, they would have compromised the British Government and would not have been disclosed.

I should mention at this point that Robert Harris was well prepared for writing the *Enigma* novel. He was interested in Bletchley Park and had reviewed some scientific books on the subject. Why did he choose to introduce a Pole in the role of a traitor when he could have used as a model for the traitor the two actual British traitors during the period covered by the book, individuals who were active in Bletchley Park and could really have burned the whole Ultra operation?

One was the notorious Kim Philby, a frequent visitor to Bletchley Park as a liaison officer of MI-6. The other was the less well-known, but well-trusted by the Russian General Staff, John Cairncross who in 1942 and in the first half of 1943 worked in Hut 3. Peter Calvocoressi denies Cairncross's presence in the area, but it is well known that Gen. Pawel Sudoplatov of the KGB confirmed the regular receipt of stolen translated German messages in the spring of 1943. Transferring detailed O.d.B. (*ordres de bataille*) of the German Luftwaffe to the Soviets just before the Battle of Kursk could have had far-reaching and unpredictable consequences because at that time Soviet ciphers were being read by the Germans, and the British knew about it. All the data which the British obtained through Ultra were passed on to the Soviets, but in such a way as to make it impossible to identify the source. Philby's and especially Cairncross's activities in 1942 and 1943 could have had serious consequences for Ultra. I think that Harris was acquainted with the autobiography of Cairncross [*The Enigma Spy,* Century Books, London 1997], but instead of choosing Cairncross as a model for the traitor in his book, he decided to invent a Polish cryptographer, in spite of the fact that he knew perfectly well that no Polish cryptographer had ever visited, let alone worked at, Bletchley. Did he perhaps think that the Katyń story would evoke more emotion in the British reader? It is unlikely because the British tried their best to ignore that horrific massacre both during and after the war. I remember the official protests against the erection of a monument commemorating Katyń in London in the 1960s. Leaving aside Harris's book—which after all is just a novel which I happen to like very much—that was not the first book to diminish the role played by the Poles in the breaking of Enigma.

I started by writing about Harris's book because in October 2001 a filmed version appeared in the British cinemas, to the annoyance of the Polish community in England. The Polish Embassy in London sent an official protest to the British media, and the Polish Section of the BBC, as well as the press, reported on the initial comments that were made with regard to Michael Apted's film. Among others, Prof. J. Ciechanowski criticized the film strongly in his review of the film for the BBC, while the renowned British historian Norman Davies did so in the press. These protests were also reported in the press in Poland.

Taking all this into account—the choice of subtitle of *Action This Day,* the "Enigma" film, and even the e-mail discussion referred to above—it is obvious that the Polish contribution to the solution of Enigma continues to be a problem for the British. Therefore, I believe it would be useful for me to review the British attitude to the Enigma story over the last quarter-century.

As few people now remember, it was not Garder, Farago, Kahn, Bertrand, or Winterbotham who disclosed the most important secret of

World War II. It was Col. Władysław Kozaczuk, then employee of the Polish Central Military Archives, who in 1967 briefly described the Polish Enigma success and also made an introductory evaluation of it in his book on the history of the Polish prewar intelligence service (the Polish Second Bureau). The book was entitled *Bitwa o tajemnice: Służby wywiadowcze Polski i Niemiecky 1918–1939* [*Battle for the Secrets: The Intelligence Services of Poland and Germany, 1918–1939*]. It has had five editions so far: in 1967, 1969, 1975, 1977, and most recently in 1999. Kozaczuk's revelations in 1967 based on Marian Rejewski's memoirs and his own good knowledge of what remained then in the archives of the Polish Second Bureau, received no notice in the West, except for Germany. Bletchley Park employees kept silent. Very few of them even knew about the Polish contribution [Cf. remarks of Gordon Welchman in his *The Hut Six Story*, M & M Baldwin, Cleobury Mortimer, 2nd ed. 1998, pp.1–2]. Nobody either in France or Germany knew that the Polish success in breaking Enigma resulted in the development by Britain and later the U.S. of an extremely powerful weapon. However, the Germans refused to accept the fact that the Poles had solved Enigma before the war. At least that was the view expressed in the journal of former Abwehr officers, *Die Nachhut* ["The Rear Guard"]. In any case, Kozaczuk's book gradually revealed the history of Enigma to the world.

In 1973, an interesting book was written by Gen. Gustave Bertrand, the prewar head of the code department of the French Second Bureau. It was entitled *Enigma, ou la plus grande énigme de la guerre 1939–1945* (Plon, Paris 1973). He wrote the book (as he states on pp. 265–67) in reaction to a chapter in Michel Garder's *The Secret War of the French Special Services 1935–1945* (Plon, Paris 1967) in which no reference is made either to Bertrand himself or to Enigma but which concentrates solely on the activities of Hans Thilo Schmidt. It cannot be said that Bertrand's book was well written or that it was a success. However, it soon became clear that the information it contained on deciphering Enigma was accurate. The French-Polish cryptological cooperation before 1939 and 1940–42 was soon disclosed (without names) as well as the ensuing successful deciphering of German codes. The disclosure was not due to Bertrand's book, however, but rather following the appearance of another book written in English, which soon became an international bestseller, namely, *The Ultra Secret* (1974) by F. W. Winterbotham. Although the description of the Ultra system in that book is accurate, the results obtained from Ultra were overestimated. Winterbotham implies that the war was won as a result of Ultra and that it is he who is responsible for having kept the Ultra secret. The book also contains irritating inaccuracies and in fact, Alan Stripp, a British codebreaker, called the book an "unrecognizable caricature" (introduction to the second edition of Welchman, 1998, p. xii). Winterbotham repeats the legend about a Polish worker who had stolen the German Enigma. Later, his attempts to defend himself by saying that he had been told the story, instead of correcting the record and admitting that it was untrue, upset not only the Poles but also such eminent reviewers of the book as David Kahn, author of *The Codebreakers* [Macmillan, New York 1967]. Kahn lost no time in naming the Polish mathematicians as being the ones who first solved Enigma. He stated that Bertrand's and Winterbotham's books were the tip of the iceberg as far as incorrect accounts of the Enigma story are concerned. In the 1970s, the British government declassified some documents on the subject of Enigma and eventually an official five-volume history of the British intelligence service was written by Sir F. H. Hinsley and others in the years 1979–88 at which time the true history of Enigma became known.

However, a special appendix in the first volume of the Hinsley synthesis [*British Intelligence in the Second World War*, vol. 1. HMSO, London 1979], "The Polish, French and British Contributions to the Breaking of the Enigma," continued to cause annoyance and protests from the Polish community living in England. Protesting also were the French historian Gilbert Bloch and even Marian Rejewski who gave a long interview to Richard A. Woytak and corrected Hinsley's version line by line for the readers of *Cryptologia*. One such objectionable statement read: "From 1934, greatly helped by a Pole who was working in an Enigma factory in Germany, they began to make their own Enigma machines" (vol. I, p. 489). Such inaccuracies were numerous and Rejewski's corrections alone filled seven printed pages. He was "increasingly disturbed by the distortions, propaganda and simple nonsense being published about the Enigma story" [R. A. Woytak in *Cryptologia,* Jan. 1982, p. 75]. We understand that some of Hinsley's mistakes were due to lack of access to the original sources or to Polish publications, but some of them were certainly the unexpected effect of the then current bestsellers, namely, Winterbotham's *The Ultra Secret* published in England, and William Stevenson's *A Man Called Intrepid* [Harcourt, Brace and Jovanovich, New York 1976] and Anthony Cave Brown's *Bodyguard of Lies* [Harper and Row, New York 1975].

Not only Hinsley was misled. Woytak noticed that "a ranking U.S. intelligence official . . . solemnly assured (him) that Cave Brown's book is an important source of new information on World War II intelligence operations." Let me state that in the last volume of his work [Appendix 30 in vol. 3, part 2, London 1998] Hinsley corrected many of the original inaccuracies and in the main satisfied those interested. Some data, however, should still be added and some passages explained more fully. In September 1939, the Polish Cipher Bureau destroyed all documents concerning Enigma and its solution for the sake of keeping it secret—historians have been the poorer for it.

Besides the bestsellers (or rather Enigma thrillers) mentioned above, serious historical studies were published by Ronald Lewin in 1978 [*Ultra Goes to War: The Secret Story,* Hutchinson, London 1978] and a Polish historian from London, Józef Garliński [*Intercept: Secrets of the Enigma War,* Dent, London 1979]. Both authors received valuable assistance from Col. Tadeusz Lisicki, the wartime superior of the Polish codebreakers Marian Rejewski and Henryk Zygalski in London in the years 1943–45. A specialist in radiocommunications, Colonel Lisicki explained fully the true story of the Polish contribution of the Enigma solution. He questioned Col. Stefan Mayer of the Polish Second Bureau who had supervised Operation Wicher. He interviewed all living Polish participants in the story. He conducted exhaustive research of archives in the Polish Institute and Sikorski Museum. He corresponded with Rejewski for many years. Eventually he became an internationally acknowledged expert. It is thanks to him that many popular articles were published in the Polish community newspapers in

London and professional reports on deciphering the Enigma appeared, such as in an appendix in Józef Garliński's book. When the first international conference on radiointelligence (SIGINT) in the Second World War was held in Bonn-Bad-Godesberg and Stuttgart on November 15–18, 1978, it was Lisicki who read one of the main technical papers. The conference was organized by two German professors, Jürgen Rohwer and Eberhard Jäckel, and it brought together leading researchers on Ultra at that time.

A valuable new work on Enigma, *W kręgu Enigmy* (*In the Enigma Circle*) written by Władysław Kozaczuk, appeared in Poland in 1979; it had been preceded by a series of articles (two in English in the *Poland* monthly (nos. 6 and 7, 1975) and one in the East German *Horizon* in 1975). But the U.S. translation of Kozaczuk's book did not appear until 1984, and it was only later that it could influence historical research on Enigma [cf. *Enigma: How the German Machine Cipher Was Broken and How It Was Read by the Allies in World War Two*. Edited and translated by Christopher Kasparek, University Publications of America, Frederick, MD 1983].

So it was not until 1982, after a five-year printing boom on Enigma, that the situation was cleared up. Poles had been usually portrayed in the media as heroes and as those who had solved Enigma, but the "bestsellers" continued to present a grossly distorted picture of their cryptological achievements. But at least in serious historical studies the true facts about them were generally given.

Following the release by the British government of several hundred thousand declassified Enigma documents in 1977, the expectation was that the Polish contribution would be proven and reports concerning their prewar and wartime cooperation with the allies made public. Nothing like that happened because only a part of the Enigma decrypts was made available by the Public Records Office, including a few summary reports from Bletchley.

One of the most favorable descriptions of the Polish contribution was popularized in a brief but valuable book written by Peter Calvocoressi, an officer of Hut 3 in Bletchley, published in 1980 [cf. *Top Secret Ultra*, Cassell, London]. However, neither he nor Patrick Beesley

[*Very Special Intelligence,* Hamish Hamilton, London 1977] added anything new to what was known about the Polish contribution. This was done, however, by Prof. Gordon Welchman, not in his excellent book of 1982 on cracking the Enigma codes, but in an article written after he had received Col. Gwido Langer's report of August 1940 (after the French campaign) ["From Polish Bomba to British Bombe: The Birth of Ultra," Christopher Andrew, ed., *Codebreaking and Signals Intelligence,* Frank Cass, London 1986]. Welchman was then able to reconstruct many previously unknown elements and to verify their trustworthiness by virtue of having been one of the chief cryptologists at Bletchley Park. He regretted that he had written his book without the knowledge of Rejewski's published articles on the solution of Enigma. Writing (in the article) about his own and Alan Turing's contribution to the creation of the British "bombe," Welchman finally produced an accurate account of the role played by the Poles. Incidentally, by giving in his book "the first complete and accurate description of the significance of [Enigma's] intricacies and of the extraordinary methods needed to break its signals" he created a proper standard by which to evaluate the Polish breakthrough in 1932 and the subsequent successes until the end of the 1930s.

For nearly a decade nothing new was made public in England regarding the Polish contribution. It is only in 1988 that a book by C. A. Davours was published in the U.S., describing the Enigma of 1932 and accompanied by a computer program. The program enabled the user to operate the original ciphering machine. In 1980, a young American historian by the name of L. Y. Gouazé wrote her MA thesis on Enigma in which she expressed her admiration for the Polish breakthrough of 1932. In 1979, Richard A. Woytak, an American historian of Polish origin, made a valuable contribution to the history of the Polish Enigma in his book on the crucial 1937–39 years. He gave an account of the early history of the Ultra operation in Poland, describing the Polish intelligence service and Polish diplomacy at the time of the appeasement policy [cf. "On the Border of War and Peace," *East European Quarterly,* Boulder, Colorado 1979]. Władysław Kozaczuk's book *W Kręgu Enigmy* appeared in the extended U.S. version in 1984, translated from the Polish by Christopher Kasparek. This book stands by itself in the U.S. and in British book markets and for many writers and historians it is a kind of Enigma Bible. It supplies a wealth of data in reconstructing the history and circumstances of the Polish breakthrough in the 1930s. It also recounts in full detail the story of the Polish Cipher Bureau before and during the war, emphasizing the achievements of the Polish cryptological team during the French campaign of 1940 and its operation in Vichy France until November 1942. Six appendices prepared by Woytak and Rejewski delved into the mathematical and technological complexities of the Polish cryptological work.

However, even the new English-language publications written by Poles or people of Polish extraction were not successful in changing the approach and tone of the British publications in the 1980s on the matter of Enigma. When in 1989 F. W. Winterbotham decided to publish his autobiography, published by Macmillan in London, the interested public expected that, with so much new information available to the author, he would add something new and valuable to the Enigma story. However, *The Ultra Spy*, was, to say the least, disappointing. Not only were previous inaccuracies not corrected, but new legends were created. It is regrettable that Winterbotham did not repeat what he had said in an undated letter to Colonel Lisicki in 1974, that is: "Firstly . . . I am not myself a cryptographer, and although Colonel Menzies, my chief, kept me generally informed of progress I knew no details. Secondly, I was not allowed to say even what I did know in my book." (quoted from a Xerox copy in my possession. Original in a London archive, Z.J.K.) Such an excuse was perhaps acceptable in 1974. But what Winterbotham made public in his memoirs in 1989 no longer was. Once again he repeated the old story in a new version. One passage is so outrageous that it is worth quoting in full. First of all we are told that he is the father of the Ultra operation. He writes that in 1939 "neither he [i.e., Commander Denniston, head of the Code Cypher Department] nor anyone else had any idea what the Germans would use for encyphering their signals." Are we to understand that the use of the Enigma machine by the German army was discovered in England thanks to our hero? Further on in the book he writes: "I asked Menzies to send a telegram to all our representatives in the Eastern European states asking for any information on the subject. The Poles were the only ones to reply to our telegram and it was from Warsaw that we began to get information on the whole subject of the German secret cypher traffic." So this is how the famous meeting at Pyry on 25 and 26 July 1939 is viewed by Winterbotham, a meeting at which the Polish Cipher Bureau, with the permission of the Polish Chief of Staff, invited the British and French specialists to present them with the reconstructed and permanently adapted Enigma machines, the result of seven years of deciphering the Enigma traffic? Winterbotham goes on to say, "The full story of how we acquired the knowledge of the Enigma cyphers did not come out until some years after the war." That is true, but what follows is a shocking inaccuracy to any reader even slightly interested in the Enigma story. He states: "Our allies, the French, had acquired a spy in the German Signal Service in Berlin, back in 1934 [in fact, in 1931. Z.J.K.]. This man had fed the French, who operated under a General Bertrand [actually a captain at that time], all the details of the Enigma machine cypher, with instructions not only on how to use it but how to construct the machines. For a while, the French Secret Service had operated by themselves, but when they wanted help they turned to the Polish Secret Service who, in turn, constructed some thirteen Enigma machines and, with the help of the agent in Berlin, devised ways of breaking the cypher." In fact, it was not the French cryptographers but the Polish representative of the Cipher Bureau, Colonel Langer, who accepted Bertrand's gift, and it was the Poles who made successful use of it. Both the French and the British cryptographers (who received the same instructions and a superficial description of the Enigma machine at the same time!) were so slow in understanding the workings of the machine that they were unable to use the received materials and did not make any progress throughout the 1930s. It was the Poles, thanks to the intuition and calculations of Rejewski, who were able to reconstruct mathematically the working part of the machine and to solve it. It is true that the Poles constructed some thirteen copies of the Enigma—the number is probably right—but it is untrue that the

137

French ever used the Hans Thilo Schmidt materials because they never read Enigma themselves, and neither did the British. The French intelligence service paid for the Asché material—the Poles never subsidized the French codes department in any way. This is not the end of the story. Winterbotham continues: "As a result, the French General Staff had been able, over the years, to establish the size and complete organization of the German army. They had not told us a word." The French intelligence worked hard on the O.d.B. of the Wehrmacht without the Enigma, and the only help they received came from regular cooperation with the Polish intelligence service, who indirectly passed on information obtained from the steady deciphering of the Enigma. It is not for me to comment on the question of whether or not the French should have shared their materials with the British. [A good recent book to consult on this question is Peter Jackson's *France and the Nazi Menace: Intelligence and Policy Making 1933–39,* Oxford University Press, Oxford 2001].

At the dawn of the war the allied ability to read Enigma is described by Winterbotham as follows: "Now, in 1939, the spy had been found and shot and all ability to read the cypher signals had been lost since the Germans had added so many more possible computations to the machine." In fact, the spy was not shot but committed suicide, and it happened not in 1939 but in 1943, when he was betrayed by a Frenchman who had been working with the French intelligence before the war. The ability to read the Enigma had not been lost—the Poles possessed the know-how—but the newly created technology for finding the Enigma keys was simply too expensive for the Polish intelligence service. Having only some indispensable bombes and the Zygalski sheets, the Polish cryptologists were able to solve only 10 percent of the keys between January and August 1939. But because the Poles knew that the allies had the resources to construct more bombes and additional sheets, they organized the giveaway meeting at Pyry in July 1939.

The Pyry meeting itself is described by Winterbotham in the following words: "It was now that at least the French came clean. [Who did not, for goodness' sake? Z.J.K.]. We sent a delegation to Warsaw, including Colonel Menzies, who posed as a mathematician, and asked

for their aid [whose aid did they ask for, from the Poles? The French?].
"A Polish model of the Enigma machine was eventually handed over to
Menzies by Bertrand on Victoria station. I saw it in our office a few
days later." Certainly it was not the head of the British intelligence
but the head of the GCCS, Comdr. A. G. Denniston, who sent a delegation to Warsaw, and this happened at the invitation of Colonel
Langer! Neither Winterbotham, nor his chief, Admiral Sinclair, sent a
delegation with Menzies. Winterbotham's "we" is a pathetic expression
of helplessness in the face of an extraordinary event, not a statement
of fact. Menzies did not participate at the Pyry meeting. I mentioned
earlier that the British team was composed of Commander Denniston
himself, his cryptologist Alfred Dillwyn Knox and the head of the
Y-Service, the psuedonymous "Commander Sandwith." Furthermore,
they did not ask (who would they have asked?) for help; they were the
surprised beneficiaries at this meeting organized by the Polish Cipher
Bureau. And it was not "a Polish model" but a genuine reconstructed
and working Enigma machine that was offered to Menzies at Victoria
station. If Winterbotham had seen it, he should have remembered the
real thing, not "a model." (All quotes from pp. 195–96).

Enough of these quotes. This long example of how the Enigma
story and its connection with the Poles has been distorted is surprising
in itself. Winterbotham's story was written anew fifteen years after *The
Ultra Secret*. If any books should be forgotten forever, *The Ultra Spy* is
certainly among them as it contains more of a mixture of truth and
invention than the previous bestseller. Nobody denies Winterbotham's
achievements as a spy in Nazi Germany and later a distributor of Ultra
information. As regards the Enigma story, he was certainly an insider,
so one could have expected accuracy in his memoirs.

Winterbotham's and other similar stories have been repeated frequently in the British popular publications. *The Big Idea*, a series of
"popular science books aimed at scientists and non-specialists alike,"
published a small volume in 1997 on the brilliant British mathematician Alan Turing. As he was connected with the process of breaking
the Enigma code during the war, a brief early history of the Ultra operation, which in fact was Enigma, is added. What we find there is so

distant from the truth as to be exceptional: a mixture of Cave Brown and the early Winterbotham stories. Here is a quotation: "The story of Bletchley begins in 1938, when a young Polish engineer called Robert Lewinski turned up at the British Embassy in Warsaw. He claimed to have worked at a factory in Germany, where they were manufacturing code-signaling machines. Lewinski had managed to commit the details of this machine to memory. He was soon smuggled out of Poland to Paris, where he supervised the construction of a machine. The British had heard about these machines, which were known as "Enigma" and were used by the German command to send coded orders to forces in the field." And further on: "Thanks to Lewinski, the British intelligence operators at Bletchley now knew exactly how an Enigma machine was constructed, and how it worked." Nobody in Poland denies the validity of Turing's achievement in 1940 in the creation of the British bombe, and if anything, such stories as this might call Turing's brilliance into question. But the whole story as recounted by Paul Strathern is simply untrue [Cf. his *Turing and the Computer*, London 1997, pp. 59–60].

Fortunately, some people in Britain do accept a true account of the facts. In a fascinating report by Stephen Harper (published in 1999) on how the HMS *Petard* seized the German naval codes in the Mediterranean in October 1942, we find an unexpected appendix on "The Polish Contribution to Breaking the Enigma" [cf. *Capturing Enigma*, Sutton, Stroud 1999, pp. 167–171]. The description of events is close to the truth. Being a professional journalist the author made proper use of the Hinsley and Kahn accounts. Among some minor inaccuracies are the date of the Pyry meeting (25 and 26 July 1939, not the fourteenth) and the description of Pyry as a small village, while in fact it was a suburb of Warsaw a few kilometers only, not twenty miles, from the center of the city. But these in no way diminish the value of the appendix. A more serious mistake is the comment that after 15 December 1938 the Poles did not read Enigma. In fact, they continued to read it but were able to do so less than before; mostly SD (Gestapo secret service) messages and very irregularly the German army traffic.

The position taken by the members of the Bletchley Park Trust in their publications [cf. "The Bletchley Park Trust Reports"] has been influential in better informing the British public. In a series of papers read publicly on various occasions, the contribution of the Poles is frequently mentioned. The papers, published in the form of inexpensive pamphlets, are meant for tourists visiting Bletchley Park. It is gratifying that they are based on existing scientific literature and sometimes on documents newly discovered in the Public Record Office at Kew. The Bletchley Park exhibitions contain a great deal of information about the Polish contribution. The Zygalski sheets have been painstakingly reconstructed (originals offered by the Polish Cipher Bureau in 1939 have as yet not been found). The first Polish Day (in fact a weekend) at Bletchley Park at the end of July 1999, on the 60th anniversary of the Polish gift to the Allies at Pyry, was a great success. British and Polish speakers took the floor and among the papers delivered there were several concerning the Polish contribution [Gallehaw, Garliński, Kapera].

Another person who gave recognition to the Poles is Capt. Hugh Skillen, an old member of the British Intelligence Corps. In his writing, which he started in 1989, we find numerous friendly references to Poles. The author of *Spies on the Airwaves* [Pinner 1989], *Knowledge Strengthens the Arm* (1990), and *Enigma and Its Achilles Heel* (1992) has used a lot of Polish material, sometimes with the help of his Polish colleague, Tadeusz Lisicki, and his French colleague, Gilbert Bloch, whose knowledge of unpublished materials (even those written in Polish) is amazing. It is thanks to the publishing and editorial opportunities offered by Skillen that the proceedings of the annual meetings of Bletchley Park veterans have appeared regularly since 1992. We also find some references pertaining to the Polish contribution to the Enigma story in the volumes published following Enigma symposia. In the latest volume of the *Enigma symposium 2001* [Pinner 2001] H. Skillen rewrites the memoirs of General Bertrand and the report of Colonel Paillole on Hans Thilo Schmidt, offering his own version of the story of the prewar Enigma and the Polish and French contributions to Operation Ultra during the war. His essay is entitled "The Four Germans who Destroyed Hitler" (pp. 12–90).

I wish to say a little more now about a new trend which was started with the book of Hugh Sebag-Montefiore, a journalist whose columns have appeared in *The Sunday Times, The Sunday Telegraph, The Observer, The Independent on Sunday,* and *The Mail on Sunday.* His book, *Enigma: The Battle for the Code* [Weidenfeld and Nicolson, London 2000], was published following his visits to Warsaw, Berlin, Paris, and Washington. He examined new material and interviewed surviving witnesses to the Enigma story and their families. H. Sebag-Montefiore was a barrister before he became a journalist and, what is more relevant, his family owned Bletchley Park before it was bought by Comdr. A.G. Denniston in the late 1930s. The Bletchley Park story has become a personal passion for him, as is clearly evident in his book. He did an enormous amount of work in preparation for his book and took the trouble, that professional historians did not bother to take, of interviewing close family members of Hans Thilo Schmidt.

Before proceeding to my comments on Sebag-Montefiore's book, I should like to stress that it contains the only fair description of the achievements of the Polish cryptologists, apart from Welchman's and Kahn's accounts. Not only does the author recognize the value of the Polish gift of 1939, but he also evaluates accurately the importance of the Polish know-how to the allied war effort. However, it seems to me that his emphasis on the character of the Enigma traitor in his book distorts the whole story.

At the beginning of the book, Sebag-Montefiore makes his approach to the Enigma story plain. He is correct when he states that all books about Enigma "have one characteristic in common. They all say that it was thanks to the brilliant codebreakers at Bletchley Park that Britain managed to read Nazi Germany's most secret messages." Sebag-Montefiore accepts that "the codebreakers did of course make a vital contribution. But they never would have achieved what they did if some of the Enigma codebooks and manuals had not been first captured by spies and ordinary British seamen who risked, and sometimes lost, their lives in the battle for the code." [cf. p. 1]. All this, including mention of "the British," is correct—a few lines down the page the author makes proper mention of the raiders, sailors of "the British, American and Canadian Navies."

The British method of breaking the German Naval Enigma was to capture "Enigma codebooks and apparatus" and subject the material obtained to analysis by the Bletchley codebreakers. However, the Swedes broke into the Geheimschreiber, which was much more complicated than the Enigma, without having to resort to the capture of an enemy vessel, but thanks only to the genius of one mathematician [cf. B. Beckman, *Svenska kryptobedrifter*, Bonniers Förlag, 1996]. It cannot be ruled out, given what happened on the Baltic Sea in 1944 and 1945, that the Soviets also broke the naval Enigma. They too had brilliant mathematicians. The British way was the fastest, but it certainly was not the only possible way of breaking the code.

We cannot exclude the fact that the Poles' perfect knowledge of the machine and the habits of the German signal men would have been very helpful if not decisive. For a full six years they had been observing and reading the Enigma day by day. The extraordinary expertise thus gained was largely put aside by British intelligence. Sebag-Montefiore quotes a few clear examples of Polish know-how being used to break the Enigma code. Of course, the Poles had only minor experience with the naval Enigma because the number of signals available to them was relatively small in comparison with Wehrmacht signals. What is more, they had not been ordered to study the naval Enigma on a continuous basis. Nevertheless, we should not forget that before breaking the Enigma code they had easily solved a major part of the German navy's codebook and had read the Enigma signals of the Kriegsmarine. This was achieved shortly after the Poles had observed some German naval exercises at the beginning of the 1930s. The Poles also had an advantage over other Allied codebreakers, and that was their strong conviction that the Enigma code could be beaten by intellectual effort alone. In the history of Bletchley Park there were periods when the codebreakers were stymied by changes in German Enigma procedures and the only solution was to capture Enigma codebooks again. In similar situations before the war, the Poles were able to anticipate the German moves.

Contrary to Sebag-Montefiore's and Bloch's contention [cf. *Enigma avant Ultra,* Paris 1990], I am not at all convinced that the material provided by Schmidt, "the Enigma spy," was decisive. Sebag-Montefiore wrote: "without Schmidt's assistance, army and air force Enigma messages would . . . never have been read regularly by the Allies before the war" [cf. pp. 1–2). This is simply not true and there is no proof for it. First of all, before the war only the Poles read, day by day, the military and non-military Enigma codes until 15 December 1938. Second, it does not appear that Schmidt's assistance was decisive, except at the very beginning, and let me turn to the opinion of a specialist in that field.

Krzysztof Gaj, a contemporary professional mathematician and specialist on the security of present-day codes is of the opinion that the decisive factor in the period from 1933 to 1945 was the reconstruction of the connections between the rotors based on the theory of permutations. He wrote: "Rejewski started his work by first analyzing the beginnings of the intercepted messages . . . [This analysis] led to a set of equations, in which permutations played the part of unknowns. Rejewski was quite right in guessing that cipher operators did not choose the three letters constituting the message key completely at random. As a result, he received a set of six equations with four unknown permutations. Those unknown permutations represented respectively:

- the internal connections of the right rotor;
- the internal connections of the middle, left, and the reversible (fixed) rotors;
- the plugboard connections; and
- the entry drum connections.

Admittedly, it is not known so far if that set of equations can be solved [cf. *Szyfr Enigmy: Metody Złamania (The Enigma Cipher: Methods of Breaking)* [Wyd. Komunikacji i Łączności, Warszawa 1989] (All quotes from his own English summary in *The Enigma Bulletin,* no. 1, Cracow 1990, pp. 63–67).

I have to rely on my memory for the following comment. Going through Lisicki's papers in mid-1990s, I saw a letter written by Rejewski at the Polish Institute and Sikorski Museum in London. In it he tried to answer the question of whether he would have been able to solve the Enigma without Bertrand's material. He was pretty sure that this was mathematically possible, but for this at least seventy messages from one day would have been necessary, and this could only have been achieved by an extraordinary stroke of luck. He thought also that the solution would have required a very long process. The question, however, kept haunting Rejewski. He even tried to check this anew, but finally he gave up.

Now we come to the evaluation of the value of Bertrand's material to Rejewski. As Gaj puts it, "The tables of daily keys had unmasked . . . (Rejewski's) third permutation, which represented the plugboard connections of the machine. The fourth permutation, however, remained a tantalizing secret. Rejewski was lucky to discover it by intuitive guessing. The set of equations obtained thus, now with only two unknown permutations, was relatively easy for him to solve."

It should be added, in connection with the mathematical analysis of one of Rejewski's published papers (containing two methods for the solution of Enigma that were never applied) that "Rejewski would have been able to solve his set of equations even if he had been supplied with only one table of daily keys for a month. He was also able to determine the permutations representing connections of the entry drum without guessing." So the element of luck which helped Rejewski in 1932 was important only in that it enabled him to find the solution faster. The final result did not depend specifically on the data provided by Bertrand. At the beginning, one month's table of keys was decisive in Rejewski's initial breakthrough, but not later when the Enigma machine had already been reconstructed.

The second reason why I do not attach much importance to Bertrand's delivery of data to Rejewski throughout the 1930s is that Rejewski received Schmidt's information only once, at the very beginning of the changes made to the German military cipher machine. With the help of his colleagues, Zygalski and Różycki, he was able to keep track of all the sophisticated changes introduced by the German experts without the assistance of Hans Thilo Schmidt's information. The last of Schmidt's supplies of Enigma tables reached the Poles probably on 22 August 1938. They were only usable through August and September 1938. What everyone forgets, however, is that even on the eve of the war, after the great changes made to the codes on 15 December 1938, the Poles were still able to read Enigma messages because they had immediately reconstructed the new fourth and fifth wheels, thanks to SD transmissions. All the changes made by the Germans could have been solved had there been more money for producing additional Zygalski sheets and more machinery, that is, the Polish "bombes." With the tools available to them, the Polish team was able to read 10 percent of German (military) messages, according to Rejewski.

Everybody who examines the list of 1939 decrypts provided by Colonel Langer in 1940 comes away with the idea that the Poles were not reading the army's Enigmas in 1939. The only break mentioned is for 26 August for the messages of 6 July 1939. Yet that view is far from the truth. Even in looking through my own private documentation I find two additional breaks. The first took place at the beginning of April and concerned the very important moment of the return of the German armed forces from the second invasion of Czechoslovakia to their barracks in Germany. The deciphered message was intercepted at 8:00 P.M. on 3 April from the military radio station at Zossen, near Berlin. Both the location of the radio station at the signal center of the German Supreme Command and the contents of the message prove that OKH signals were read at least occasionally. Available data enables us to establish that the break was achieved in one day, i.e., it took much longer than in 1938 when deciphering normally took a few hours only; however, it was still relatively fast.

It is not clear and needs elucidation if the passage in Woźny's book quoting for the first time the message of 3 April is an original translation from the German or simply a summary of the report, but it is evident that the data contained in the message is genuine and the hour of interception is noted. The document is available at the Central Military Archives of the Polish army, No. GISZ I 302.4.643 [cf. A. Woźny,

*Niemieckie przygotowania do wojny z Polską w ocenach polskich naczel-
nych władz wojskowych w latach 1933–1939.* (*Nazi Miliary Preparations
for War with Poland in the Judgment of the Polish Supreme Military
Authorities in 1933–1939*) Neriton, Warszawa 2000, p. 260].
The second successful break occurred most probably on 26 August
1939 and it concerned the messages of the previous day. According to
the 29 April 1940 report of Maj. Maksymilian Ciężki, at the beginning
of a few messages of 25 August an abbreviation was noticed confirming
the full mobilization of the German army. This abbreviation was known
to the Polish Second Bureau well in advance. Even before the messages
of the day in question were eventually deciphered, this information was
at once passed on to Ciężki's superiors. Unfortunately for the Poles, all
orders concerning the concentration of the German army were sent to
the troops not by radio but in another way, so the gain from the deciphered messages was "not specifically worth noticing," according to
Major Ciężki. In any case, we can say that the Polish cryptologists were
still able to break into the army's Enigma messages with the tools available to them. However, they did so irregularly and with only a small
delay (on the next day). Ciężki's report is to be found at the Archives
of the Polish Institute and Sikorski Museum in London at Ref. No.
BI.bl/3. (I should like to express my thanks to Mr. A. Suchcitz for
bringing this report to my attention and for making it available to me
for study.)

That was the last prewar break, according to Ciężki, but it proves
once again that the Poles kept track of the changes in the Enigma
machine and Enigma procedures. Once again it should be stressed that
it was the Polish team who, with a sufficient number of Zygalski sheets,
were able, on 17 January 1940, to resume reading Enigma (in the
presence of a British codebreaker). Solving the Enigma code required
more than an answer to the question of the order of characters on the
machine's keyboard versus the standard typewriter keyboard, which
was so fervently sought by Alfred Dillwyn Knox. The British at
Bletchley Park received all the necessary sheets in mid-December
1939, and yet they were unable to start deciphering for a month. It
shows that it was know-how that was most helpful in new breaks. This

fact is emphasized several times in Sebag-Montefiore's *Enigma*. It is the only monograph, aside from what was written by the cryptanalysts, that gives proper recognition to the Polish contribution.

The British were grateful to the Poles for sharing their knowledge of Enigma codes and codebreaking, and allied cooperation in this respect was very successful. Until the end of the French campaign, only 18 percent of daily breaks were made by the Poles, but it should be noted that the small Polish team, in accordance with the wishes of the French army authorities, concentrated first of all on deciphering all intercepted Enigma messages. That was regrettable as they could only attempt to make further breaks in their spare time. As Sebag-Montefiore stresses, the fact that the Poles shared all their information with the British at the beginning of May 1940 was frequently a decisive factor in solving the next important change in German code procedure when the Germans stopped double encryption of the first three letters at the start of the message. The ability to read the changed Enigma code this time came about as a result of an idea of John Herivel, a young British mathematician. The so-called Herivel tips were decisive in 1940 and for this all the credit goes to the British codebreakers.

The basic technical data obtained from the Poles by the British was also fundamental to their success with the four-wheel Naval Enigma. On the basis of all newly available data, including two postwar reports on the activity of Hut 8 at Bletchley Park (i.e., the recently declassified documents: (1) Patrick Mahon, "The History of Hut 8, 1939–45; and (2) Hugh Alexander, "Cryptographic History of the Work on the German Naval Enigma"), Sebag-Montefiore estimates that without the Polish contribution, the breaking of the Naval Enigma would have been delayed until as late as December 1942!

In summary, I should like to quote something that is obviously pertinent but not yet properly understood. In a letter to Colonel Lisicki dated 5 June 1976, Rejewski observed very accurately that "while in the years 1932–33 paper and pencil were enough to solve the Enigma, later on a cyclometer was necessary, then (cryptological) bombes and (perforated) sheets, but what was necessary next, that can be told in the best way by the British." Now we are told by Sebag-Montefiore that the capture of Enigma documents was the decisive factor. I agree that that is so with regard to the breaking of the naval Enigma codes, but generally speaking this is not a correct evaluation of the code-breakers' work at Bletchley Park. The importance of American intercepting devices and the hard daily effort of everyone working at Station X has been stressed, all of which is very true. But the cryptologists were on the front line and without their work and their achievements there would have been no work for others. It is equally true that without Rejewski, the whole success with Enigma would not have been possible. Behind him stands the forgotten figure of Col. Gwido Langer, head of the Polish Cipher Bureau, the *spiritus movens* of the Polish Enigma enterprise.

CONCLUSION

In the period between the initial declassification of Enigma documents and the beginning of the twenty-first century, we have observed the following typical choices being made by British authors writing about Enigma:

1. *Minimizing the Polish contribution* by inventing the figure of a Polish engineer (of Jewish origin, for some reason) whom the Polish intelligence service put in touch with Major Gibson, the representative of MI-6 in Warsaw in 1938, to help him sell his knowledge of the Enigma machine to the British (unaccountably in Paris). This was the story produced by F. W. Winterbotham in 1974 and Anthony Cave Brown in 1975 as well as their many followers. From time to time we find the same story resurfacing even now (see Strathern's pamphlet on Turing).

2. *Presenting half-truths or near-truths,* such as the subtitle of the book *Action This Day*, which did not garner much favor from the Poles. Fortunately, the contents of the book are fairly accurate. L. Kruh's observation was right when he stated that "full

credit is given where it belongs" (meaning to the Poles). It would be appropriate if minor inaccuracies were to be corrected in footnotes to the next edition.

3. *Telling the truth.* Here we should list former codebreakers starting with Gordon Welchman and his colleagues. Some of them decided to write what they knew and to make it public. One example is Hugh Foss, who concluded his report on his prewar work on Enigma by saying that at Pyry "the Poles . . . gave us the complete answer." In fact, in evaluating the British prewar attempts to decipher Enigma, he expressed the opinion, in his account of the Allied meeting in Paris in January 1939, that "the Poles . . . must have considered us all very stupid." This is how he viewed the difference in levels of achievement in reconstructing the cipher machine. However, that was not the opinion of the Polish cryptographers. Before the Pyry meeting, they had been forbidden to share their secret. They came to the Paris conference anxious to obtain suggestions that would enable them to continue their work. Eventually, left to their own devices, they battled on by themselves with just 10 percent of the necessary technical equipment. As I mentioned before, in spite of these difficulties, the Polish codebreakers were able to decipher Enigma again and again. However, by July 1939 they were happy to share all their knowledge with the Allies. They knew that continuing to decipher Enigma on a daily basis and in large volume exceeded the resources available to them. They continued working until their last days in Warsaw and were able to restart their deciphering work again in France in January 1940. The British took over after the fall of France.

Our friends who share our view of the value of the Polish contribution are watching for any new declassified documents that could shed new light. Here I should like to express my thanks to Ralph Erskine for supplying a few pages of an unpublished report on the deciphering of Enigma by Turing. Some historians are starting to include the main events of the Enigma story in their publications. I should like to mention, first of all, G. Weinberg's synthesis [*A World of Arms: A Global History of World War II*, Cambridge 1993] of the Second World War in which the Polish gift to the Allies in July 1939 is given its due. The relevant passage reads as follows:

"In July of 1939 the Polish codebreaking experts, with the approval of their government, turned over to the French and British duplicates of Polish reproductions of the German Enigma machine used for encoding radio messages. By this step and related ones the Poles made a major contribution to the whole Allied war effort, which has tended to be obscured by the excessive award of credit to themselves in French and British accounts of what came to be known as the 'ultra' secret." The U.S. historian's work has been published by the Cambridge University Press. Nothing of this kind has appeared in British historical works of the last decade.

4. *The staff in Bletchley Park have been trying to establish the whole truth* about the Polish contribution and to make it known to the public. Here I wish to mention once again the paper read by John Gallehawk (later published separately) and his publications, found in archives and museums. Not only is the Polish community in the U.K. grateful to Bletchley Park for its work and publications in this regard, but so are all Poles, both in Poland and abroad.

The most recent step in the proper direction, that is recognition of the Polish contribution, has been the unveiling of the Enigma memorial at Bletchley Park on 12 July 2001. The special ceremony was attended by the Duke of Kent, who is the official protector of the Bletchley Park Trust. Apart from the British representatives, of particular importance was the presence of the close relatives of the three Polish mathematicians, members of the Polish diplomatic corps, representatives of Polish organizations in the U.K., and World War II veterans.

The ceremony, which preceded the Bletchley Polish Festival of 2002, was a great success, particularly in the eyes of the

Polish community in England. Emerging from near oblivion, although not present in person, were the three people who had broken the Enigma and made operation Ultra possible: Marian Rejewski, Jerzy Różycki, and Henryk Zygalski, who broke the Enigma code and created a basis for Operation Ultra. In fact, they were present in spirit at the exhibition, but the Poles needed to commemorate them officially, especially at Bletchley Park.

The monument is in the form of an open book lying on a broken table, representing the fact that the Polish mathematicians broke the Enigma code and made the reading of German messages possible. The book is sculpted in bronze and the table in granite. The artist of the monument is Prof. Szańkowski of the Academy of Fine Arts in Warsaw. The unveiling of this monument was made possible thanks to the cooperation of the Polish Union, the British authorities and, above all, the friendly attitude of the Bletchley Park Trust representatives. The funds came in large part from private donors and were raised by the Polish London daily, *Dziennik Polski*.

The date of this event coincided with the seventieth anniversary, in December 2002, of Rejewski's breakthrough and the start of the Polish Operation Gale, which preceded Ultra. I view the recent article by the well-known British historian, Michael R. D. Foot, on Rejewski and the breaking of Enigma [cf. *Rzeczpospolita*, June 13/14, 2002, pp. A10–A12] as a turning point in the approach taken by British historians to the Polish contribution. The sooner the British authorities decide to release further documents concerning Enigma and Ultra, the better will truth and justice be served.

Judging from all that has been written about Enigma, it appears that the breaking of the Enigma code remains vivid in the memory of our contemporaries. After a quarter of a century of scientific and historic research on Enigma, it seems that we are still at the beginning. There are many facts that have not as yet been checked, many questions unanswered; many documents are missing and few are really available. It is amazing that the Enigma secret has been kept by so many people for nearly thirty years. It is unfortunate and hardly amusing that the British authorities continue to withhold all the pertinent documents. This allows for the creation of new myths and legends such as those in the Harris book and the Apted movie. Data on the early years of Allied cooperation on Enigma survive only in the British archives. Allowing free access to them now should be a priority. Some of the people who were involved are still alive. Evidently the greatest war of the last century is not forgotten and people continue to be interested in the splendid achievements of their fathers.

Jagiellonian University

Index

THE ENIGMA BULLETIN

Edited by Zdzisław Jan Kapera

No. 5 - June 2000   ISSN 0867-8693

The Enigma Press, ul. Borsucza 3/58, 30-408 Kraków, Poland; E-mail: zjkapera@vela.filg.uj.edu.pl

The Enigma Bulletin

Series edited by Dr. Zdisław J. Kapera (Jagiellonian University) since 1990.

ISSN 0867-8693

Distributed by:

The Enigma Press
ul. Podedworze 5
32-031 Mogilany, Poland
zjkapera@vela.filg.uj.edu.pl

Our potential subscribers from the United States are requested to order back and current issues from:

Classical Crypto Books
P.O. Box 1013
Londonderry, NH 03058-1013, U.S.A.
CryptoBooks@aol.com

All back and current issues are available in England from:

M & M Baldwin
24 High Street
Cleobury Mortimer
Kidderminster DY14 8BY, England
mb@mbaldwin.free-online.co.uk

World War II History from Hippocrene Books

Fighting Warsaw: The Story of the Polish Underground State, 1939–1945
Stefan Korbonski, Introduction by Zofia Korbonski

> "Absorbing, inspiring . . . The book, which is detailed and written with humor, modesty, and a surprising lack of rancor, makes it quite plain that there is an indomitable quality in the Poles." —*The New Yorker*

Fighting Warsaw is an extraordinary human story. Stefan Korbonski, the leader of the Polish Underground State, portrays the years of the German occupation during the Second World War, and the beginning of anti-Soviet underground activities thereafter. His story presents the entire organization, strategy, and tactics of the Polish underground, which included armed resistance, civil disobedience, sabotage, and boycotts. This new edition contains an introduction by his wife, Zofia, as well as 16 pages of previously unpublished personal photographs.

508 pages • 5½ x 8½ • 16-page b/w photo insert • ISBN 0-7818-1035-3 • $14.95pb • (594)

Did the Children Cry? Hitler's War Against Jewish and Polish Children, 1939–1945
Richard C. Lukas, Foreword by Norman Davies

Based on eyewitness accounts, interviews, and prodigious research by the author, *Did the Children Cry?* is a unique contribution to the literature of World War II, and a compelling account of German inhumanity towards children in occupied Poland. Winner of the 1996 Jausz Korczak Literary Competition.

263 pages • 5½ x 8¼ • 16 b/w photos • ISBN 0-7818-0870-7 • $14.95pb • (44)

The Enigma of General Blaskowitz
Richard Giziowski

An extraordinary biography of a German army commander, Johannes Blaskowitz, who dared to question Hitler's atrocities.

532 pages • 6 x 9 • maps • ISBN 0-7818-0503-1 • $29.95hc • (141)

Forgotten Holocaust: The Poles Under German Occupation, 1939–1945, Expanded Edition
Richard C. Lukas, Foreword by Norman Davies

Since its first publication in 1986, this book has become a classic of World War II literature. The revised edition includes a short history of ZEGOTA, the underground government organization working to save the Jews, and an annotated listing of the many Poles executed by the Germans for trying to shelter and save Jews.

358 pages • 5½ x 8½ • ISBN 0-7818-0901-0 • $14.95pb • (291)

The Murderers of Katyn
Vladimir Abarinov

Originally published in 1991, this book represents the first comprehensive attempt by a Soviet journalist to reveal the truth behind the murder of 15,000 Polish Army officers in the Second World War.

250 pages • 6 x 9 • ISBN 0-7818-0032-3 • $19.95hc • (520)

The Forgotten Few: The Polish Air Force in the Second World War
Adam Zamoyski

While rarely remembered today, some 17,000 men and women passed through the ranks of the Polish Air Force while it was stationed on British soil. They played a crucial role in the Battle of Britain in 1940, and they also contributed significantly to the Allied war effort.

272 pages • 6 x 9 • illustrations/maps • ISBN 0-7818-0421-3 • $24.95hc • (493)

Poland in World War II: An Illustrated Military History
Andrew Hempel

"A notable amount of information is offered in a small package."
—*Polish-American Journal*

Poland's participation in World War II is generally little known in the West. In actuality it was not an easy victory for the Germans in 1939, and after the conquest of Poland, the Poles continued to fight in their homeland, on all European fronts, and in North Africa. This illustrated history presents the Polish military war effort, intermingled with factual human interest stories.

120 pages • 5 x 7 • 50 b/w photos/illus./maps • ISBN 0-7818-1004-3 • $9.95pb • (484)
120 pages • 5 x 7 • 50 b/w photos/illus./maps • ISBN 0-7818-0758-1 • $11.95hc • (541)

Poland's Navy, 1918–1945
Michael Alfred Peszke

Created in 1918 when Poland regained its independence after 123 years of foreign domination, the Polish Navy fought in World War II alongside the British Royal Navy. This book analyzes the history and unique contribution of the Polish fleet.

220 pages • 6 x 9 • photos/illus./maps • ISBN 0-7818-0672-0 • $29.95hc • (770)

Pearl Harbor: Japan's Fatal Blunder, Illustrated Edition
Harry Albright

"A fascinating history of the raid with some ingenious speculations about what might have been."   —*Los Angeles Times*

In a gripping narrative accompanied by photographs, author Harry Albright reviews the decisions made by the Japanese strike force commander and examines the battle of Midway in this light. He also considers what a third attack on Oahu might have accomplished.

378 pages • 5½ x 8½ • 16-page b/w photo insert • ISBN 0-7818-1018-3 • $14.95pb • (376)

Also from Hippocrene's Military Library

Spies & Spymasters of the Civil War, Revised & Expanded Edition
Donald E. Markle

". . . a marvelous book. It weaves an intertwined yet easy to understand perspective of people, places, organizations, secret societies, politics, and the vehicles of spy craft during an unprecedented time of upheaval in our country's history."
—*The Midwest Book Review*

Now expanded with a chapter on American espionage after the Civil War! This book covers the entire history of Civil War espionage for both the Union and Confederate armies. The activities and tactics of hundreds of spies are described, including spymasters who controlled spy networks, like Allan Pinkerton, Lafayette Baker, and Generals Dodge, Sharpe, and Garfield. The book also examines the role of special groups, such as the Negro underground organizations and women spies. Drawings and photographs of key figures are included.

560 pages • 6 x 9 • 8-page b/w photo insert • ISBN 0-7818-1037-X • $14.95pb • (622)

Lost Victories: The Military Genius of Stonewall Jackson
Bevin Alexander

"A delightful work; fascinating and provocative and well-written."
—*Roanoke Times & World News*

While studies of the Civil War generally credit Robert E. Lee with military expertise, this account argues that Stonewall Jackson was a superior strategist who could have won the war for the South: Had Lee accepted Jackson's plan for an invasion of the North, the South might have surprised and dismayed the Union forces into defeat. Using primary sources, Bevin Alexander reconstructs the battles that demonstrate Jackson's brilliance as a commander, including Antietam, Fredericksburg, and Chancellorsville. Detailed maps accompany this controversial account of a pivotal moment in American history.

350 pages • 6 x 9 • ISBN 0-7818-1036-1 • $14.95pb • (614)

Gettysburg: Crisis of Command, Illustrated Edition
Harry Albright

> "Succeeds in giving the reader an insider's glimpse of . . . the decisions that shaped the course of the battle and the future of these United States."
>
> —*Marine Corps Gazette*

This historical narrative of America's greatest battle examines the course of events and the tensions within the two armies' commands. Harry Albright argues that poor decisions and disputes on both sides nearly led to disaster for each. The book makes events clear to even the reader unfamiliar with the strategic and tactical elements of armed combat on a grand scale.

300 pages • 5½ x 8½ • 16-page b/w photo insert • ISBN 0-7818-1039-6 • $14.94pb • (640)

Korea: The First War We Lost, Updated Illustrated Edition
Bevin Alexander

> "Fast moving . . . superb."   —*Library Journal*

> "Well researched and readable."   —*The New York Times Book Review*

Now in its fifth printing, *Korea: The First War We Lost* has become the definitive reference in its field. In a preface to this edition, the author reflects on the road from the war of the 1950's to the early twenty-first century, and the threat of a volatile Korea with nuclear potential.

560 pages • 6 x 9 • 80 b/w photos/illus./maps • ISBN 0-7818-1019-1 • $22.50pb • (661)

Lightning in the Storm: The 101st Air Assault Division in the Gulf War
Thomas Taylor

> "The ultimate Gulf War memoir. The reader is there, feeling the desert heat, the excitement, and the adrenaline rush of war. It doesn't get any better than this."
>
> —*Library Journal*

This account delivers a gripping portrayal of the 1991 conflict with Iraq. As the only air assault division in the world, the 101st Airborne Division played a crucial role in Operation Desert Storm. This is their story, based on dozens of interviews and hundreds of army videos. This compelling account of modern warfare delivers suspenseful battle scenes, clear explanations of strategy, and fully developed portraits of many of the combatants.

470 pages • 6 x 9 • 16-page b/w photo insert • ISBN 0-7818-1017-5 • W except UK • $19.95pb • (407)

Prices subject to change without notice. **To purchase Hippocrene Books** contact your local bookstore, call (718) 454-2366, or write to: HIPPOCRENE BOOKS, 171 Madison Avenue, New York, NY 10016. Please enclose check or money order, adding $5.00 shipping (UPS) for the first book and $.50 for each additional book.